WAY
BUT LOVED

WAYWARD BUT LOVED

*A Commentary and Meditations
on Hosea*

Ray Beeley

THE BANNER OF TRUTH TRUST

THE BANNER OF TRUTH TRUST
3 Murrayfield Road, Edinburgh EH12 6EL
P.O. Box 621, Carlisle, Pennsylvania 17013, USA

© 2001 Ray Beeley
First published 2001
ISBN 0 85151 797 8

Typeset in 11/12.5 pt Garamond at the
Banner of Truth Trust, Edinburgh
Printed and bound in Finland
by W S Bookwell

Contents

Foreword   vii

Introduction   1

1. The Marriage to Gomer   11
   Chapter 1:1–9

2. The Gracious Promise of Restoration   23
   Chapter 1:10–2:1

3. Israel's Unfaithfulness   27
   Chapter 2:2–13

4. Hope of Restoration   38
   Chapter 2:14–23

5. The Patience of Restoring Love   49
   Chapter 3:15

6. The Controversy of God with His People   55
   Chapter 4:1–14

7. The Lord's Warning to Judah   67
   Chapter 4:15–19

8. Proud Israel Is Defiled   73
   Chapter 5:1–9

9. 'They Will Not Listen!'   83
   Chapter 5:10–15

10. An Exhortation to Repentance   89
    Chapter 6:1–3

11. 'What Shall I Do?' Is God Ever Puzzled?   94
    Chapter 6:4–11a

12. 'The Pride of Israel Testifies to His Face!'   104
    Chapter 7:1–16

13. 'Set the Trumpet to Your Mouth!'   118
    Chapter 8:1–14

14. The Threat of Captivity   128
    Chapter 9:1–9

15. 'The Withering Away of Israel'   135
    Chapter 9:10–17

16. 'A Twig on the Water!'   143
    Chapter 10:1–10

17. Urgent Appeal and Solemn Warning   154
    Chapter 10:11–15

18. God's Love and Israel's Ingratitude   163
    Chapter 11:1–7

19. God's Pity   172
    Chapter 11:8–11

20. Ephraim Condemned, Judah Warned   178
    Chapter 11:12–12:14

21. The Evil Calf Worship   191
    Chapter 13:1–3

22. The God of Grace Will Act in Wrath   196
    Chapter 13:4–11

23. Disaster and Deliverance   201
    Chapter 13:12–16

24. Israel's Conversion and Renewal   207
    Chapter 14:1–9

Notes on Authors Cited   221

Foreword

It is perhaps customary for believers to put '*soli deo gloria*' somewhere, usually at the end of their work, but I would like to make it my starting point. It reflects my sense of gratitude to the Lord for the knowledge to which he has brought me of his great salvation, for the light he has given me upon his Word, and for the personal sense of his mercy through the Lord Jesus. His Word has indeed been a lamp to my feet and a light to my path, and I hope these studies express something of its relevance and excitement to me through the years. In a way, this book celebrates my experience of over fifty years as a Christian – a continuing proof of the divine mercy of which Hosea speaks so richly.

There are many people here on earth, and not a few now in heaven, to whom I owe thanks. Among the latter is my father, in whom I first saw the reality of gospel faith, and Doctor Lloyd-Jones, who showed me great kindness in a few occasional personal meetings and whose preaching deeply affected my theology. Still on earth are many others, not least my wife, who has supported me, coping with my books and funny ways for approaching fifty years. She also typed the original manuscript of these Hosea studies some thirty years ago, and I lovingly dedicate this book to her.

Many, too numerous to mention by name, have helped me and prayed for me. Their faithful consistency over many years has been a source of continual encouragement and a testimony to the covenant faithfulness of the Lord, whose grace has made us his own. My daughter Susan, nearby in Sheffield, and my son David, in Gateshead, are also worth a mention as a source of encouragement.

I am especially grateful to Iain Murray for his encouragement to put Amos and now Hosea into book form. Both started life as handwritten studies for the encouragement of young people in the Bible class at my home church.

There are special thanks, too, for those who have helped and encouraged me with Hosea: Dr Hywel Jones and the editorial staff at Banner have, by their editing, produced order out of chaos. Robert and Barbara Storrie assisted with the original cover design and title. I am also grateful to all who have contributed to the arduous task of tracing sources and quotations, especially Miss Brenda Dixon of Sheffield University, who has diligently employed her librarian skills in this respect, and the Rev. David Cartledge of the United Free Church at Milngavie. Both have been friends 'beyond the calls of duty'.

Supremely, I hope that readers will join me in rejoicing in the tender love and abiding faithfulness of our great and glorious God, the faithful husband of his covenant people, whose grace guarantees that the fallen are not forsaken and persuades us that 'though wayward, we are eternally loved'.

RAY BEELEY
January 2001

Introduction

Dates

Hosea, the prophetic successor to Amos, prophesied to the Northern Kingdom of Israel in around 750–723 B.C., the period immediately before its demise in 722–721 B.C.

Political background

To appreciate Hosea's message we must understand Israel's historical background. God had called Abraham and delivered the Hebrews from bondage in Egypt through Moses. Under Joshua's leadership they had settled in Canaan, the land God had promised them. Through the nation Israel God would fulfil his promises that the seed of woman would bruise the serpent's head (*Gen.* 3:15) and that all the other nations would be blessed (*Gen.* 12:3). But from the beginning the Israelites singularly failed to exercise the faith and obedience which would have brought rich blessing. The prophet Jeremiah later spoke of 'the kindness of their youth and the love of their betrothal' (*Jer.* 2:2), referring to the wilderness period, when they were free from the religious influence of other nations. But even there they often failed to trust God, as is shown in the history contained in Exodus, Leviticus, Numbers and Deuteronomy. After the death of Joshua came a period of religious decline, during which the existence of the nation was preserved only by divine intervention by a series of judges, culminating in Samuel, who was both judge and prophet. At this time the people demanded a king to be like other nations, in spite of Samuel's warnings. What resulted was the disastrous reign of Saul and the Philistine oppression. God in his grace raised up David to be their deliverer, and for a time the kingdom prospered under him and his son Solomon.

The later years of Solomon saw decline and drift towards idolatry through the king's many political alliances. These years also saw the surfacing of deep tensions between Judah and the rest of Israel, tensions which had existed in the reign of David but had been successfully calmed by him. The northern tribes deeply resented Solomon's concentration of government, wealth and resources in Jerusalem and the burden of forced labour required by his many building projects there. They also resented the attempt to centralise worship in the new temple in Jerusalem.

Jeroboam, an Ephraimite, emerged as leader of the unrest. He had been exiled by Solomon, but on Solomon's death he returned from Egypt to confront Solomon's son and successor, Rehoboam. The responding heavy-handedness of Rehoboam, however (*1 Kings* 12:1–15), culminated in full rebellion and the establishment of a breakaway northern kingdom called Israel, or Ephraim. Judah, the southern kingdom, remained loyal to the house of David. The writer of the book of Kings points out that behind this was the sovereign purpose of God, to chasten an increasingly apostate people (*1 Kings* 11:33).

To secure his position in the Northern Kingdom, Jeroboam set up an alternative system of worship to that of the temple in Jerusalem. Still using the name of the Lord, he placed calf images at Dan, in the north, and Bethel, in the south of his kingdom. An increasingly debased form of Jehovah worship developed which included many of the religious practices of Canaan and the surrounding nations. This contravened the divine purpose that Israel should be a spiritually unique people through whom God would reveal himself to the nations. Jeroboam's death led to a period of political instability and deepening religious corruption which, in spite of the ministry of Elijah, came to a head in the reign of Ahab and Jezebel. The Lord brought the dynasty of Ahab to an end, but there was no real turning back to God, although Elisha, Elijah's prophetic successor, laboured long and faithfully to that end.

The most significant ruler of the new dynasty was Jeroboam II. His arrogance is suggested by his choice of throne name, which commemorated the one who first made Israel to sin (*1 Kings* 16:26). His reign of about forty years was a time of unparalleled wealth in Israel, but it was also a time of great materialism and religious decline. It was during these years that Amos and Hosea began to prophesy. Hosea's earliest oracle foretells the downfall of the house of Jehu, to which Jeroboam belonged.

Although Judah remained faithful to the house of David and maintained the worship of the Lord in the temple in Jerusalem, the kingdom was far from blameless, as is shown in Hosea 6:4, 11; 8:14; 10:11; and 12:2. The messages of Isaiah and Micah, who prophesied to Judah a little later than Hosea did to Israel, give details of this. Even so, Judah enjoyed periods of religious reform in the reigns of Asa (911–870 B.C.), Jehoshaphat (873–848 B.C.), Uzziah (790–740 B.C.) and Hezekiah (729–686 B.C.).

Assyria, to the north, began to emerge as a great power, and it was only a matter of time before its attention was drawn to Palestine with its small and relatively vulnerable states. The prophets were aware of the hand of God behind the political scene, and Isaiah proclaimed that Assyria was to be the rod of God's anger against his unfaithful people (*Isa.* 10:5). The Assyrian empire had been quiescent during the reign of Jeroboam II. But in 745 B.C., Tiglath Pileser III (Pul) became king, and soon Assyrian expansion began to threaten the very existence of the Palestinian kingdoms.

At this time Israel was entering a period of political instability in which a succession of rulers perished through violence or political intrigue. In 743 B.C. Zechariah, the son of Jeroboam II, was murdered after a six-month reign; Shallum, his murderer and successor, perished after only one month. Shallum's murderer, Menahem, reigned for about five years, but Menahem's son Pekahiah was murdered after a two-year reign by his army commander, Pekah. Five years later Pekah himself was murdered in a revolt led by Hoshea, who then became king.

The Assyrians would probably have put an end to the kingdom of Israel at this time, had not Hoshea surrendered to become tributary to Tiglath Pileser. When Tiglath Pileser died, Hoshea revolted with Egyptian help. It was three years before the new Assyrian king, Shalmaneser V, was free to open up an all-out assault on the Palestinian territories. Hoshea was captured, and Samaria, his capital, was besieged for three years. Shalmaneser died before the city was taken, but his successor, Sargon II, brought the siege to a successful conclusion. Samaria was completely destroyed in 721 B.C.

Hosea roundly condemns the policy of hovering between alliances with Egypt and Assyria (7: 8–12). His prophecies reflect vividly the political intrigue, murder, bloodshed, religious apostasy and the general breakdown of law and order in the last days of the Northern Kingdom. It is likely that the prophet did not live to see the final downfall of Samaria, since he makes no reference to it.

Religious background

When the Jews first settled in Canaan the strongest factor in their national unity was their religion, which expressed their unique relationship to the Lord. This covenant relationship demanded an exclusive allegiance to the Lord and complete separation from the Canaanites. Their failure to observe their covenant responsibilities exposed them to the temptations of a corrupt heathen civilisation. They learned much about agriculture from the Canaanites, whose practices were bound up with religious fertility rites and the worship of the pagan Baals (the word means 'lord' or 'owner') and the female consort,

Ashtaroth or Astarte, to whom the fertility of the land was attributed. There were many such Baals, but all were regarded as local manifestations of the one great Baal and his consort.

Since the fertility of the land was ascribed to the sexual relations of the Baals and their consorts, it is not surprising that Canaanite worship was highly sensual and erotic and included immoral acts unthinkable under the strict moral code of the law of Moses. This was highly attractive to the sensual inclinations of the people. Many corrupted their worship of the Lord with the idolatry of Baal worship and the debased festivities of the fertility cults.

The typical pagan sanctuary was located on a high place with an open courtyard in front of the shrine. In this roofless court stood the altar for animal sacrifice and beside it a stone pillar, representing the god, and a wooden pole or pillar, representing the female deity. To these sanctuaries individuals and families came with their gifts. During great agricultural festivals crowds of people gathered for occasions which gave rise to drunkenness and every kind of debauchery – all carried on, ostensibly, in the name of the Lord. This is the background against which the prophecy of Hosea must be understood.

This worship comprised four main features:

1. It was akin to magic, in that its aim was to control the god for man's own purposes.

2. It deified the process of reproduction and led to licentious behaviour.

3. Its main concern was material blessing.

4. Its ritual was divorced from any sense of moral obligation.

All this has undoubtedly a very contemporary ring. Hosea knew what it was to be in conflict with a permissive society.

The prophet

Hosea and Amos were near contemporaries, prophesying in the Northern Kingdom of Israel during the long and prosperous reign of Jeroboam II (783–746 B.C.). It is generally accepted that Amos, who was from Judah, was the earlier of the two and that Hosea's ministry began in the later part of the reign of Jeroboam, which has often been spoken of as Israel's Indian summer. The introductory verse of Hosea's prophecy indicates a ministry extending over some thirty years. It is not known whether the two prophets ever met or whether Hosea ever heard Amos prophesy, but it is possible that he knew something of his message. The strict justice so evident in the prophecy of Amos had more tender overtones in the love and compassion of Hosea. There may be some analogy in the complementary nature of the ministries of John the Baptist and the Lord Jesus Christ.

From the prophecies we may draw the following conclusions about the character and personality of the man:

1. He had an intimate knowledge of God and appreciation of his covenant love, with a deep awareness of the practical implications of this (4:1).

2. He was warm-hearted, full of compassion and pity (11:8).

3. He was deeply emotional and worked under great stress. We see this in abrupt transitions of thought, repetitions and powerful language (chapter 11).

4. He had a keen sense of observation and an imaginative approach to the world of nature. Pictures drawn from nature and the everyday life of the countryman appear again and again. It has been suggested that he may have been a farmer or a baker before he was called to be a prophet (10:11; 7:4–8).

5. He was intelligent and cultured enough to show understanding of the political intrigues of the day (12:1).

6. He had a good knowledge of biblical narratives up to this time (10: 9; 12:3–4; 12–14).

7. He was fully aware that the source of his message was the Lord. He knew that he was not just a man attempting to speak on God's behalf, but that he had been called and sent by God to proclaim his message (11:9; 13: 4–5).

His personal background

Though we have no record of the prophet's call, we have more information about the personal background of Hosea than of most other Minor Prophets, and we can see how profoundly, in the providence of God, his domestic experience coloured his whole message.

Chapters 1 and 3 are mainly biographical. They are concerned with the prophet's experience with Gomer, his unfaithful wife. Scholars are not agreed as to whether Gomer was a prostitute before marriage. Indeed, some have even argued that this part of the book must be read symbolically, since God would never command one of his prophets to associate with an immoral woman. But the story is presented as a narrative, and the law placed restrictions only on priests in terms of their marriage partners. Some commentators have suggested that God directed Hosea to marry an immoral woman who already had illegitimate children, since that would reflect Israel's relationship to God from the beginning. Others have suggested that Gomer was not a harlot at the time of her marriage, but God knew that she was inwardly corrupt and would prove unfaithful. In any case, the immoral wife and the illegitimate children demonstrate Israel's apostasy. The divine command to Hosea to seek Gomer out in the slave market and buy her back vividly depicts the divine love and the ultimate triumph of redeeming grace. When all the false lovers have forsaken Israel and despise her, God will love her still.

The prophet's own life sheds clear light on God's method of revealing himself. He does so not only by disclosing truths in words (that is, propositional revelation), but in the course of events and the context of relationships. In Hosea we have an Old Testament revelation of the truth that God is love (*1 John* 4:16). That lesson was learned by Hosea in the school of his own personal tragedy. We may imagine the anger and bitterness of his outraged love, which was entitled to divorce, and his desire to try to forget the woman who had proved so unfaithful. Yet he found the grace of God constraining him to a higher way. He became possessed and dominated by a love which would not be quenched but which, having renounced all self-pity, would persevere in self-giving until the wayward one was redeemed. Hosea's experience was to embody the abiding covenant love of God for his wayward people. No wonder James Montgomery Boice, in his *Expositional Commentary on the Minor Prophets (Vol. 1)*, calls this 'the second greatest story in the Bible'. In depth it is surely exceeded only by the expression of the love of God for sinners in the incarnation, life, atoning sacrifice and resurrection of the Lord Jesus Christ.

The sin of Israel

The prophecy reveals a deeply spiritual conception of sin.

1. It was primarily an affront of love. God had desired their loving response to his grace, but they had withheld this (6:6). The problem went much deeper than broken law; it was a matter of heart affection. Faithlessness was in their very nature and expressed in their idolatry (5:4).

2. The monarchy of the Northern Kingdom embodied the infidelity of the people and reflected the sin of Gibeah (9:9; 10:9). The reference here is to the story contained in Judges 19–21, when the tribe of Benjamin was almost exterminated for its ungodliness. It should also be noted that Saul, the first king of Israel, came from the tribe of Benjamin and his birthplace was Gibeah (*1 Sam.* 10:26; 11:4). Hosea seems to have regarded the monarchy of the Northern Kingdom as evil in itself, and it is significant that in 253 years, no fewer than eighteen kings from ten different dynasties had occupied the throne (8:4; 9:15).

3. The nation was looking in the wrong direction for security. They busily sought political and military alliances instead of seeking the Lord.

4. Their failure to love God had led them astray. They had turned from the divine law, misled by their priests who had failed to instruct them in the truth. Consequently they had debased the worship of the Lord their God and had set their hearts on that which was self-indulgent and morally evil. Baal worship epitomised this with its idolatry, prostitution and preoccupation with material blessings.

5. They had put on a show of repentance which did not arise from the heart (6:4–6).

The covenant love of God

Over against the sin of the people, Hosea exalts the covenant love of God.

Hosea's love for Gomer reflects the far more wonderful divine original, God's love for his people in the face of their rebellion. The love of Hosea with its long-suffering patience and acceptance of personal disgrace depicts the wonder of the divine love for sinners in the cross of the Lord Jesus Christ.

Two Hebrew words give the key to this relationship. The first is 'knowledge' (*da'ath*). This is not a factual or conceptual awareness but is experiential, a knowledge born of personal communion, loving contact and deep experience (cf. *Amos* 3:2). 'To know' is to meet, converse, share experience, make response, disclose and commit oneself. God himself has made a commitment and requires a responsive commitment from his people. Hosea 3:3 implies that from the recipient's point of view this means a total surrender. The other is 'covenant love' (*hesed*). This signifies a steadfast love which pledges itself and will not let the other party go. It often refers to the love of God for his people, but it may also be used of their response to him. When referring to God, it reveals tensions in his heart which surpass the highest capacities of human understanding and for which human language is entirely inadequate. God is holy; punish sin he must. But he is also love; and cease to love, he will not.

His invincible love will find a way to redeem and purify his most unworthy people. The final chapter of this prophecy anticipates Calvary and the gift of the Holy Spirit at Pentecost, exalting the sovereign grace of the Redeemer's love.

The people you love best can hurt you most, but it is the nature of the divine love not merely to chasten and rebuke, but to redeem and restore.

The text of the prophecy

The text of Hosea presents the student with special difficulties.

It is not as well preserved as the bulk of the Old Testament, and as a result, a number of scholars have resorted to extensive emendation. This is unwise, since in general the Massoretes were careful in transmitting the text. Even the vowel pointings, which were inserted only in the sixth to ninth centuries A.D., should not be lightly discarded. Some amendments may be necessary, but these should be done with great caution.

The oracles were preached at various times and then brought together on one scroll. It is not always easy for us to discover the editorial principles on which the collection was finalised.

The emotional nature of the prophet and the stress under which he spoke have left their mark on his language. It is not always easy to analyse exactly, but the sense is clear.

The prophet refers to some contemporary events, the significance of which is lost to us.

However, the prophecy of Hosea, as part of the Holy Scripture, should be studied prayerfully and with great care. The Holy Spirit, the ultimate author of all Scripture, will give understanding to those who are ready to be taught by him. For those who will study prayerfully and attentively, the book will yield powerful and edifying lessons.

Chapter 1:1–9

The Marriage to Gomer

Verse 1: **The word of the LORD.** This is not a word from man about God, but God's own word about himself through a man (see *2 Pet.* 1:21). The emphasis is on:

1. The sovereignty of God. The word came in God's way, at God's time.

2. The authority of the word. As it is the word of God, it has all the abiding qualities of the author. Since he is the Lord of the universe, it is a word of absolute authority. Since he is Lord of the nations, it is a word of absolute power. Since he is eternal and unchanging, this word has abiding value. Since he is the faithful covenant-keeping God, the word brings hope to a people who would otherwise have been without hope.

The Word is truth (*John* 17:17).

The Word is power (*Eccles.* 8:4, *Rom.* 1:16).

The Word of God abides for ever, and the life which it begets is eternal (*1 Pet.* 1:24).

The security of God's people rests in the unchanging nature of his grace (*Mal.* 3:6). This is the great lesson of Hosea's prophecy.

To Hosea. The revelation was personal. In the very name of the prophet there was hope, for it means 'salvation'. The fact that God was pleased to reveal himself through men indicates his tender regard for mankind, whom he created to have fellowship with himself and to whom he continues to speak, in spite of their rebellion and sinful blindness towards him. This process culminates in the Word who was made flesh and dwelt among us (*John* 1:14).

The son of Beeri. Of the prophet's family we know nothing at all, but his pedigree is not important to the revelation. This is a truth confirmed by Paul's teaching that grace does not run in the blood. Its saving light is not dependent on human qualifications (*1 Cor.* 1:26–28).

V2: **When the LORD began to speak by Hosea.** The first lesson God had to teach through Hosea was by means of his relationship with Gomer. In a different way, it is still true that God speaks through our human relationships, so the Apostle Paul teaches that Christian marriage should mirror the relationship between Christ and his church (*Eph.* 5:22–33).

Wife of harlotry (NIV: 'adulterous wife'). Commentators are divided in their understanding of this phrase. Some suggest that Gomer became immoral only after her marriage. Others follow Matthew Henry's explanation that it refers to her scandalous behaviour before marriage.[1] Those who accept this point of view argue that it reflects strongly the grace of God to Israel as a nation called out of idolatry. It may be suggested that only from actual experience would the prophet begin to understand the nature of the forgiving love of God about which he was to speak. Calvin, E.W. Hengstenberg and E.J. Young take the first chapter as a symbolical vision, believing that God would not command his prophet to unite himself with an immoral woman.

Nothing in the text suggests that it should be read any way other than literally, but it is not necessary to assume that Gomer was already an immoral woman at the time of her marriage. Many commentators take the phrase to mean that she was already tainted with the sinful inclinations so generally

---

[1] This and other comments of Matthew Henry are taken from his *Commentary*, of which various editions are currently available.

attributed to the people at this time, though not yet a prostitute at the time of the marriage.

The figure is consistent with what we know of the people of Israel: while still in the wilderness, they began to show themselves unfaithful to God, lusting for the meats of Egypt (*Exod.* 16:3) and committing adultery with the daughters of Moab (*Num.* 25). If Gomer was already a prostitute, the redemptive aspect of the analogy is brought out even more strongly, since he had first to make an honest woman of her. This resembles God calling Abram out of the idolatry of Ur of the Chaldees. Whenever he calls people, it is out of the darkness of sin.

Children of harlotry (NIV: 'unfaithfulness'). If Gomer was already an adulteress, the children may be those she already had by other men. It is pointed out that in 2:1 the plural 'sisters' is used, although only the one daughter, Lo-Ruhamah, is mentioned in chapter 1. We are also reminded in Genesis 1:24 that each produces after its kind, and this applies in the spiritual as well as in the natural realm. It is no wonder that the law speaks of the iniquity of the fathers being visited on the children to the third and fourth generation (*Exod.* 20:5). An ungodly example aggravates the problem already present in fallen nature. It is no surprise that the children of Gomer were called children of unfaithfulness, begotten as they were in immorality by an immoral woman. Verses 6 and 8 make no mention of Hosea in connection with the children, Lo-Ruhamah and Lo-Ammi, indicating that they were probably illegitimate.

The land has committed great harlotry *by departing* **from the Lord.** This is explained in length in the rest of the book. Hosea's family is used as a divine visual aid.

V3: **So he went.** The obedience of the prophet should be noted. Though forewarned of the painful consequences that would follow, he immediately and unquestioningly obeyed. We should not speak of this as blind obedience. This was the obedience of a truly seeing faith, reaching out beyond the immediate circumstances and resting in the character of God. It is the Holy One who gives the orders, and we are assured that his purposes are always, at last, for the good of his children.

Gomer. The name has been taken to mean 'a burning coal' or 'completion'. Some commentators have taken it to signify 'burning with lust' or one 'near to destruction'; others suggest that it refers to the final accomplishment of the purposes of love in spite of her initial rebellion.

Diblaim has also been taken symbolically. Meaning 'bunches of dried figs', it has been taken to indicate God's purpose that Israel should be fruitful. We should, however, be careful of reading too much into symbolic meanings of names where these are not explained in the text.

V4: **Jezreel.** The name has a double meaning: 'the Lord will scatter', or 'the sowing of the Lord'.

The prophecy uses both meanings to indicate, first of all, the Lord's judgement (verse 4), and then his blessing (verses 10–11). In 2 Kings 10:11, Jezreel is where the descendants of the family of the wicked king Ahab were slaughtered by Jehu (*2 Kings* 9:16, 25, 33; 10:11, 14, 17).

Some scholars create a tension between what is said here by Hosea and the account of 2 Kings 9:6–10 and 10:30, but the difficulty can be explained. When Jehu was told by the prophet Elisha that he would be king, the circumstances were most peculiar. The prophet himself did not perform the ceremony of anointing but sent a messenger, who was told to run as soon as his mission was completed (*2 Kings* 9:3). This indicated that although Jehu was appointed, it was as an executioner. There was no divine approval of him and no guidance given as to how he should fulfil his task. The blessing of 2 Kings 10:30 may be understood either as wages for the discharge of a duty, without reference to the manner in which it was carried out, or as a constraint of mercy that he should henceforth walk in obedience to the Lord. Hosea 1:4 shows how the Lord holds Jehu responsible for the cruelty with which he carried out his commission. The punishment of the house of Omri, to which Ahab belonged, was indeed divinely ordained, and Jehu was the divine instrument, although the way in which he carried it out was not acceptable to the Lord.

The book of Habakkuk and Isaiah 10:5–6 and 12 indicate the same principle of God calling to account instruments that he uses in judgement. God's work is to be done in God's way. Even the ungodly are responsible to God and will be judged according to the light of the moral law which he has given to all.

Some commentators have understood the promise of 2 Kings 10:30, that Jehu's house should endure to the fourth generation, to mean that the nation was under judgement (see *Exod.* 20:5). Since they had chosen to follow godless rulers, God would now give them such rulers. It should be pointed out, however, that Jeroboam II was the third of the house of Jehu to rule over Israel and that during his reign the nation enjoyed considerable temporal blessing in spite of its sinfulness. In the reigns of Jeroboam II's grandfather, Jehoahaz, and his father, Joash, God had shown mercy (*2 Kings* 13:4; 14–19). Even in wrath God had remembered mercy (*Hab.* 3:2). Truly the mercies of the Lord are past finding out (*Rom.* 11:33) and are beyond human efforts to explain. The godly must bow and confess, like Eli, 'It *is* the LORD. Let Him do what seems good to Him' (*1 Sam.* 3:18).

V4c: The prophet announces that the overthrow of the house of Jehu will begin the weakening process that will culminate in the complete overthrow of the Northern Kingdom.

V6: **Lo-Ruhamah** means 'not pitied'. The basis of God's dealings with Israel had been pity (*Isa.* 63:9), and for this reason he had long delayed the judgement which they richly deserved. But

[15]

because they had continually abused his grace, it would be withdrawn (*2 Kings* 15:29; 17:3–5).

V7: **Have mercy.** The verb is from the same stem as the Hebrew noun for 'womb' and indicates the tender love of a parent for his or her child. The same verb is found in Isaiah 49:15: 'Can a woman forget her nursing child, and not have compassion?'

Judah. There seems to be a contrast between God's dealings with Judah and with Israel, though some commentators have suggested that the Hebrew could be understood to mean that Judah also is not to be pitied. It is stated in 5:5 that Judah also stumbles, but it should be noted that at this point Judah had not sinned as persistently as Israel. There was in Judah a discernible remnant of grace. Some of its kings had led reformations, and the reign of Hezekiah would see a remarkable deliverance from the Assyrians just after the end of the Northern Kingdom (*2 Kings* 18–19).

Not . . . by bow, nor by sword or battle. These weapons were the things in which Israel had trusted and in which men are inclined to put their trust. We are reminded that the Lord does not depend on these (*2 Cor.* 10:3–5). Such a deliverance as this is recorded in 2 Kings 19:35–36.

Matthew Poole suggests that the contrast between Israel and Judah is deliberately drawn to abate the pride of Israel and constrain a remnant to repentance.[2] John Calvin remarks: 'He [Hosea] sets the worship at Jerusalem in opposition to all those superstitions which Jeroboam I had first introduced and Ahab increased, and all their posterity followed.'[3] He adds that Hosea

---

[2] This and other comments of Matthew Poole are taken from his *A Commentary on the Holy Bible, Vol. II* (Edinburgh: Banner of Truth, 1990), and are found under the appropriate verse headings.

[3] In *Minor Prophets, Vol. 1* (Edinburgh: Banner of Truth, 1986). Subsequent comments from Calvin are taken from the same volume and are to be found under the appropriate verse headings.

is in no way approving of the apostasies which were beginning to make inroads into the religion and life of Judah and against which the prophet issues warnings in other places (4:15; 5:10, 12, 13; 6:4, 11; 8:14; 10:11).

V8: Gomer bore a second son, whose name is also typically significant.

V9: Lo-Ammi means 'not my people' and indicates God's final rejection of the Northern Kingdom. The covenant promise of Exodus 19:5 is therefore revoked. Though the prophet continues to call the people to repent, he is aware that they will not respond.

In this section we see a progressive severity in the judgement: verse 4 speaks of punishment, verse 6 of the withdrawal of grace, and verse 9 of the final rejection.

FOR MEDITATION

1. Outline for chapter 1:
   a) The *proclamation of God.* This is God's Word, not the message of a man.
   b) The *pollution of the nation* is expressed through Hosea's wife and children.
   c) The *pain of the prophet* demonstrates the grief of God with his people.
   d) The *punishment of the nation* is expressed in the names of the children.

2. Hosea went because he was sent. We may compare him with Paul, who was not disobedient to the heavenly vision (*Acts* 26:18). There is no other adequate reason for being God's messenger. The call of the preacher is not a call from the church, though the church is usually instrumental. Still less is it a human

fancy. To preach is a solemn responsibility: No man should undertake this on any authority less than that of God himself, nor should he go in any strength other than his. Consider that the Lord Jesus Christ himself said, 'The word that you hear is not mine but the Father's who sent me.' How much more careful, then, must we be as to the source of our message! Consider Paul's words in 2 Corinthians 4:1–7.

3. V2: *So he went.* It is a matter of supreme importance that the Christian should be obedient. Psalm 123:1–3 should reflect our attitude. There should be no looking back. Consider the lessons on discipleship in Luke 9:57–62 and 14:26–27, 33.

We must:

a) count the cost;

b) renounce every other loyalty;

c) continue unwaveringly in loyal commitment.

Our determination, devotion and defence should mirror Psalm 71:16: 'I will go in the strength of the Lord GOD: I will make mention of Your righteousness, of Yours only.'

4. Vv 2–3: Consider how the relationship between God and his people is expressed through the analogy of marriage. The New Testament expounds this in terms of the relationship between Christ and his church (*Eph.* 5:22–33):

a) the deep personal love involved (*Gal.* 2:20);

b) the complete mutual commitment (*Matt.* 16:24–25);

c) the resultant union (*Gen.* 2:24, *Rom.* 6:2–5, *Col.* 3:3);

d) the abiding relationship (*Matt.* 19:6, *John* 10:27–29; 15:1–11);

e) the grace of the divine choice, that God in Christ stoops so low to make us his own (*2 Cor.* 8:9);

f) the faithfulness of God (*Deut.* 1:6, 8, *1 Cor.* 1:8–9, *2 Tim.* 2:13);

g) the purity required (*2 Cor.* 11:2).

Knowing these things should inspire us to real confidence in our relationship with God in Christ, since it is built on the unchanging faithfulness of the divine love (*Jer.* 31:3, *Isa.* 26: 3–4).

The spiritual ideal set out here should inspire us to seek to make our marital relationship reflect the divine reality, something which calls for continual dependence on divine grace. It reinforces the fundamental nature of the requirement that believers marry only 'in the Lord' (*1 Cor.* 7:39).

5. Vv 2–3: We must consider the nature of sin as prostitution. It is an abuse of the divine love when men are faithless, rebellious, and self-centred. It means that what belongs to God is used in the service of another. The title 'Baal' could carry the sense of 'the boss'. The ties of love have been sacrificed for the bondage of a slave. Though we do not worship the Baals literally, our hearts may still be tainted by this sin of offering allegiance to other lords. Christians should cast off all such distracting allegiances and acknowledge with gratitude the wonder of the divine love in the words of Robert Murray M'Cheyne:

> *Chosen not for good in me,*
> *Wakened up from wrath to flee,*
> *Hidden in the Saviour's side*
> *By the Spirit sanctified,*
> *Teach me Lord, on earth, to show,*
> *By my love how much I owe.*

6. Vv 2–3: We are challenged to consider also the sovereign nature of the divine love. God chooses us knowing our sins and defects: he elects not on the basis of his foreknowledge of our love and obedience, but in spite of his foreknowledge of our sinful rebelliousness.

7. At the human level, we have a lesson here in what God intends marriage to be. In Hosea's patient loyalty to Gomer we see what

it means for a man to 'cleave' to his wife. Remember that divorce is, at best, because of the hardness of man's heart (*Matt.* 19:8). God's answer to a marriage under strain is not divorce, but the seeking of his grace. It is God's opinion of contemporary attitudes to marriage and sex which our generation needs to see demonstrated in word and example in the lives of believers.

8. V4: Human beings are accountable to God. Though it was a long time before the sin of the house of Jehu was called to account, the accounting did come at last. So it will be for all mankind. Hebrews 9:27 reminds us of an inescapable assize; and 2 Peter 2:9 and 3:9 remind us that though the Lord is long-suffering and patient, judgement will come at last.

Amos 1–2 remind us that even the heathen nations are answerable to God. The same lesson is found in the book of Habakkuk and in many other Old Testament passages. It is made very clear in Romans 1:18–32 that part of this judgement is seen when a nation is left to itself and its sin and becomes increasingly corrupt. Perhaps we do not appreciate as we should the fact that God presently exercises his restraining grace in human society so that the immediate effect of human wickedness is limited. There will inevitably be a day of accounting!

We need to ask ourselves about our responsibility before God within our society for such evils as the pollution of the environment, abortion, victims of abuse, and neglect of those who suffer. In a democratic society surely a Christian voice should be heard speaking in accordance with the word of God. Should Christians remain passive if measures are introduced which further limit any specifically Christian contribution to our educational system? We cannot ignore the concern of the prophets for social righteousness. God's people should be lights of the world (*Matt.* 5:16). Our children may reap the fruits of our indifference.

9. V4: The nation as a whole was held responsible for the sins of the house of Jehu because they had been consenting to them. We must watch against sinning by consent. This may happen as a result of fear, laziness, or indifference. We have seen the eroding effect of ungodliness in our society in such issues as homosexuality, the laws governing marriage and divorce, and the treating of crime as sickness rather than sin. How are we to fulfil our responsibilities as the people of God in such an age?

10. V6: God does not indulge sin in his own people, though he is always ready to forgive where there is real sorrow and repentance. He will surely call to account those called by his name but who persist in walking in their own way. An outward profession of religion is not an insurance policy! Whilst the Scriptures emphasise the covenant faithfulness of God to the weakest believer who hangs upon him, there are also solemn warnings, lest security lead to presumption. The prayer, 'Search me, O God, and know my heart . . . see if *there is any* wicked way in me' should be continually upon our lips (*Psa.* 139:23–24).

11. V7: The deliverance of Judah would be by grace, not by human effort, as was demonstrated in due time in the experience of Judah under King Hezekiah. Later the Lord told the returned exiles through Zechariah that deliverance would come 'not by might nor by power, but by My Spirit' (*Zech.* 4:6). We need to be continually reminded that our salvation is by grace alone (*Eph.* 2:8–9). Psalm 115:1 reminded Israel: 'Not unto us, O LORD, not unto us, but to Your name give glory, because of Your mercy, because of Your truth.'

12. V9: *Lo-Ammi.* It spelt the end for the nation when the Lord said, 'You are no longer my people.'

In spite of the Northern Kingdom's apostasy from its beginning, the Lord had been very gracious to them, granting the blessings of the ministries of Elijah, Elisha and other lesser prophets, as well as numerous deliverances from famine and from enemies. The reign of Jeroboam II had seen considerable material blessing, but there had been no repentance in spite of the warnings.

The covenant people had sinned away their day of grace, and the contemporary church should take warning from this. Hebrews 2: 1–4 warns of the dangers of neglecting the message of salvation. Such warnings are present in Scripture not to discourage us and fill us with fear and foreboding, but to stir us out of indifference and to put an end to any tendency to false security.

The gospel of grace should make us diligent in making our calling and election sure (2 Pet. 1:10). In Matthew 7:21–23, the Lord Jesus Christ solemnly warns that many will claim that they have called upon his name but will be told to depart and will have no part in his kingdom. He completes the warning with the parable of the wise and foolish builder. The wise man who builds on rock is the one who hears the Word and puts it into practice. The exhortation of 2 Corinthians 13:5 is very important: we must examine ourselves, on the basis of God's Word about the Lord Jesus Christ and his personal indwelling in our hearts, to be sure that we are 'in the faith'.

Chapter 1:10–2:1

The Gracious Promise of Restoration

Even in the midst of wrath, God remembers mercy (*Hab.* 3:2). Judgement deserved is surpassed by mercy undeserved (*Rom.* 5:15–17). Even in dealing with the apostate Northern Kingdom, God would not break the covenant promise to Abraham.

V10 may be interpreted in three ways:

a) It is suggested that a number of members of the Northern Kingdom were re-united with Judah and restored to their own land on the return of the captives from Babylon in 537 B.C. It is clear from 2 Chronicles 30:5–20 that some from the north escaped from the Assyrians and later joined with Judah in the reformation of Hezekiah. One may justifiably argue that this was but a small fulfilment of a prophecy that surely requires fulfilment on a far greater scale.

b) It is held that the prophecy anticipates a widespread return of the Jews to a lively faith in God through the gospel. It is compared with Ezekiel 37 and Romans 11 and has yet to be fulfilled.

c) Some have argued that the fulfilment is spiritual. Matthew Poole says: 'Though the ten tribes be for ever captivated, yet God will have His Israel . . . not Israel after the flesh . . . but the Israel of God according to faith, the spiritual seed of Abraham, consisting of both Jews and Gentiles.' Calvin argues from Romans 8:24 for a similar conclusion. James' use of Amos 9:11–12 at the Council of Jerusalem (*Acts* 15:16–17) may be used to justify this spiritual approach.

The last part of the verse is another play on the name Jezreel, which may mean either 'the scattering of God' or 'the seed of God'. The judgement was to demonstrate the scattering, but in the ultimate work of grace, the seed would be seen, the sons of the living God. Where sin had abounded, grace would abound much more (*Rom.* 5:20).

V11 speaks of the gathering together of Judah and Israel, portrayed at length in Ezekiel 37:15–28, emphasising the power of grace transcending the evil brought by sin. The unity brought about by divine grace is then expressed in their appointment of one head, as consenting to the divine purpose.

One head. There is no mention of the house of David, but that is stated in 3:5. The later prophecy in Ezekiel 37:15–28 sheds more light on this hope.

The division of the kingdom was the direct historical consequence of Solomon's pretensions to grandeur and the foolishness of his son Rehoboam. But spiritually the division demonstrated the nation's apostasy from God. The people had rejected not only the house of David but also the sanctuary appointed by God in Jerusalem. They turned to worshipping the Lord after the patterns of the Canaanite religions and even to worshipping the Canaanite Baals themselves. The promise of the restoration of the house of David represented a return to a theocratic kingship, to be personalised in the Messiah, the son of David. Compare with this such prophecies as Amos 9:11 and Isaiah 9:1–7 ('Galilee of the Gentiles').

The day of Jezreel. The promise of restoration is now expressed in the change in name of the children. 'Ammi' means 'my people', and 'Ruhamah' means 'having obtained mercy'. Calvin argues from Romans 9:24–25 that this includes the Gentile seed.

FOR MEDITATION

1. Outline for 1:10–2:1, as it is completed in the New Testament:
   a) A *relationship broken* by sin: the names Lo Ammi and Lo Ruhamah.
   b) A *restoration wrought* by grace: the new names, Ammi and Ruhamah.
   c) A *reformation completed* by the Lord Jesus Christ (*1 Pet.* 2:9–12).

2. The primary thought of the chapter is the superabundance of grace. In the very place of judgement will be an even greater outstanding demonstration of the grace of God. This great truth is argued by the Apostle Paul in Romans 5:15–21. It is realised historically at the cross, where the place of judgement becomes the place of salvation. To echo the old hymn, it is 'beneath the cross of Jesus' that the believer must take his stand. There is no other hiding place from sin and shame (*Gal.* 3:10, 13).

3. *Sons of the living God.* The spiritual fulfilment is found in John 1:11–13, where it is made clear that those who have received Jesus, whether Jew or Gentile, are born of God, not of natural descent, nor of human decision, or a husband's will. The relationship is wholly the gift of God, offered by grace and received by faith.

4. The question is asked, 'Are there few who are saved?' (*Luke* 13:23). Here is the scriptural answer: they will be 'as the sand on the seashore'. The doctrine of election does not mean that only a small number will be saved; rather, it guarantees their multitude.

5. *One Head.* The Lord Jesus Christ is the one divinely appointed Head of the church. The church is his body. Our unity as

Christians must first of all be established in the Lordship of Christ in our lives as individuals. In the light of this, we must ask ourselves serious questions:

Is Jesus really Lord of my life?

Am I bound, as I should be, in fellowship with other Christians?

Does the fellowship I belong to reflect the Lordship of Christ in its doctrine and behaviour?

The spiritual fruitfulness of the Christian church begins in the spiritual transformation of the individual believer. This will lead on to fruitful soul-winning in the church of the Lord Jesus Christ. We have an example of this in chapter 1 of Paul's first letter to the Thessalonians. When they saw how the apostle lived among them (verse 5) they were so transformed that they became a model to others (verse 7), who were drawn to the truth and to the Saviour.

Chapter 2:2–13

Israel's Unfaithfulness

It has been suggested that this section is a collection of edited oracles, but there is no doubt of a common theme running through them.

V1: **Sisters.** The plural supports the idea that Gomer already had children when she was married to Hosea because only one daughter, Lo-Ruhamah, is mentioned in chapter 1.

V2: The word rendered 'plead' in KJV generally has the forensic sense of 'bring a charge against', as is reflected in most modern versions. Poole comments: 'You that have any resentments for your father, debate, or at least deal here plainly with . . . your mother and say how little right she hath to be called my wife, and how little reason I have to own myself her husband.'

She *is* not My wife. Not because he had divorced her, but because she herself had abolished the relationship by her fixed intention of going after other lovers (as is mentioned in verse 5).

Nor *am* I her Husband. By her behaviour she had forfeited all right to his love and support.

Let her put away her harlotries. The same verb is used in Genesis 35:2, when Jacob commands his children to put away strange gods. In Joshua 7:13, on the occasion of the sin of Achan, it is used when God commands Israel to put away the accursed thing. It is also found in Joshua's final speech about putting away strange gods (*Josh.* 24:14, 23) and in 2 Kings 17:23 of the

Lord's putting away of the rebellious people of the Northern Kingdom. Repentance involves the casting aside of anything that takes the place of the Lord.

Adulteries from between her breasts may indicate either:

a) that her heart was set upon her lusts;

b) that she must forsake the shameless behaviour which drew back at no wantonness to obtain what she wanted;

c) a command to remove her adulterous lovers from her affections.

V3: **Lest** implies that even at this stage there was room for repentance because of the great forbearance of God. What appears to be a final threat of judgement was even then an occasion of opportunity for repentance (see *Rom.* 2:4 and *2 Pet.* 3:9).

Strip naked. Sometimes this indicates degradation, as in the case of Joseph (*Gen.* 37:23) and that of Saul, when he fell into the hands of the Philistines (*1 Sam.* 31:9). Here it plainly includes the idea of reducing to beggary. It was prophetic of what was to happen to the rich women of Samaria (cf. *Amos* 4:1–3.). The great wealth and luxury enjoyed by Samaria under Jeroboam II would be completely stripped away. Archaeological finds have confirmed both the great wealth of the city and the terrible nature of its destruction at this period in its history.

Expose her, as in the day she was born. This probably refers to the beginning of Israel as a nation, redeemed originally from the hopeless bondage of Egypt. That the nation was chosen when in utter poverty is reflected in Deuteronomy 26:5–9, which records the confession to be made on the annual presentation of the first fruits.

Wilderness; dry land; slay her with thirst. The imagery is reminiscent of what Israel had been at the beginning of her national life when, but for the grace of God she would have perished in the wilderness. It also pictures the spiritual state of the nation, having forfeited the divine grace and 'forsaken the fountain of living waters' as did Judah later (*Jer.* 2:13). In Jeremiah 17:5–7 the same sort of imagery describes the man who does not trust the Lord.

V4: **Children of harlotry** described a people not only born in immorality but also addicted to it. Their children were being born into a society in rebellion against God, enjoying its idolatry. They, in their turn, would become delighted participants in the sins of their parents.

V5: **Their mother** refers to Israel, the nation. God was speaking here to the people, but it is plain how the experience of Hosea with Gomer suitably reflected the case between the Lord and his people.

I will go after my lovers. As Gomer had turned away from Hosea to go after other men, so the nation had turned away from God, deliberately choosing to go after false gods.

Who give *me* my bread. Here was a double tragedy: Israel was attributing her material blessings to the false gods she was worshipping, and she was completely pre-occupied with material blessings. The curse of materialism did not begin with the Industrial Revolution! It is an abiding disease of the human heart. Remember Lot's wife (*Luke* 17:32) and Jesus' parable of the rich fool (*Luke* 12:16–28). Here is a great danger for the church in the West today. Perhaps for you and me?

V6: **I will hedge up your way.** Here we see the immeasurable perseverance of the divine love, to bring home the awfulness of sin. Since Israel would set no bounds to her lusts, the Lord would impose bounds upon her so that she would not be able to indulge them (see *Deut.* 4:25–31). We see also the calculating intensity of the Lord's discipline: a love that cares enough to hurt in order to bring repentance. Some commentators see here a prophecy of the extremely stringent siege of Samaria that preceded the downfall of the city in 721 B.C.

She cannot find her paths. The frustration of Israel in the paths of self-will is reflected in Jesus' parable of the Prodigal Son (*Luke* 15:13–16). In Jeremiah 17:5 the man who 'makes flesh his strength' and 'departs from the LORD' is likened to 'a shrub in the desert'.

V7: **She will chase her lovers.** It was foreknown by God that at first the discipline would only intensify the quest of self-will after false hopes. The nation would bend all her energies in the pursuit of false gods.

But not overtake them. All the desperate efforts would be fruitless until at last she would come to her senses. Frustration can be a powerful incentive to repentance.

I will go and return to my first husband. Compare 'I will arise and go to my father' (*Luke* 15:18). Realising at last the benefits enjoyed under the gracious hand of God, Israel will again turn to him. Calvin comments that the faithful are not made wise unless they are well chastised; he regards the prophet as speaking here not of the reprobate, but of the remnant seed.

V8: **She did not know** (NIV: 'acknowledge'). 'She did not realise that all she had came from me.' This was not ignorance brought about by lack of instruction, but the ignorance of deliberate blindness of the sinner who refused to see (*Eph.* 4:18). The Lord had been providing abundantly for the nation, yet his gifts had been dedicated not to him, but to the Baals.

V9: Since Israel did not acknowledge that her blessedness came from God, she must learn the hard way. The Lord would take back these gifts by famine, pestilence and the Assyrian scourge, as had been threatened (*Deut.* 28:38–40). Should we not discern something of the disciplinary hand of God in some of the modern problems of disease, famine, and pollution?

Take away is a strong verb, suggesting plucking away by force.

Given **to cover her nakedness.** Ezekiel 16:1–8 describes how God had covered the destitution of the nation's previous plight in Egypt by his gracious favours.

V10: Her shame would be exposed for all to see, so that even her lovers would despise her. We are reminded of the utter inability of the false gods to alleviate her plight and the despicable nature of Israel in the sight of the allies she so eagerly sought after. Here was a nation utterly bankrupt, materially and spiritually.

The wonder of the divine love is emphasised here. The lovers whom she had sought so eagerly would despise her. But the Lord, so sinned against and rejected, continued to love in spite of all that she was and all that she had done. The grace of God is for the utterly unworthy (*1 Tim.* 1:15, *Rom.* 5:6, 8).

No one shall deliver. None could; none would, *but God.* (*Eph.* 2:4)! When the Lord purposes, who can overthrow it (*Isa.* 14:27)? The Almighty God is also the God of infinite grace.

V11: **Mirth.** C.F. Keil associates this with the great festivals of Passover, Pentecost and Tabernacles. Calvin associates it particularly with the external pomp which was with them, the guise of religion. It may be that the whole courtly process of roistering and drunkenness typical of Samaria's lifestyle may be in view here. The religious festivals had become occasions of vice and immorality like those of the Canaanites and the other heathen nations. No longer were the festivals occasions for self-examination and seeking after God, governed by the understanding of his holiness, but occasions for vice and unrestrained self-indulgence. One is reminded of the way Christmas is 'celebrated' today.

Appointed feasts. Though they had turned away from God, they continued to hold the religious festivals with all the trappings – in fact, with more trappings than ever! This may refer to the festivals instituted by Jeroboam at the beginning of the Northern Kingdom, which were in their very nature apostate (*1 Kings* 12:32).

'**Her**' is repeated four times, as though to draw attention to the fact that these were not the festivals appointed by God, even if their dates and times did coincide with the divinely ordained festivals. Israel's religion was self-willed, self-centred and self-ordained. It carried no divine mandate or approval.

New Moons. The first day of the month was kept as a special holy day.

Sabbath. The weekly Sabbath, the seventh day, ordained by God as a day of rest.

Appointed feasts. The great annual festivals of the Jewish religion. All these would be made to cease because they perverted true religion. This theme of perversion is common to all the great eighth-century prophets (see *Hos.* 6:6, *Amos* 5:21–24, *Isa.* 1:10–20). The same truth was emphasised by their successors (e.g. *Jer.* 7).

V12: **I will destroy.** The thought is repeated that all the wealth of the land, God's gift in the first place, would be taken away. Instead of being gratefully received from his hand they had been regarded as rewards for false worship, as though their false gods were their benefactors!

I will make them a forest. The cultivated groves and vine-yards would become wild and desolate through pillage and depopulation.

The beasts of the field shall eat them. No one would remain to defend them and to carry on the processes of husbandry. This indicates how severe the judgement would be: people and property alike would be destroyed. Such was the seriousness of their sin. Jeremiah later speaks of the feigned repentance of Judah (*Jer.* 3:10). The same thought is doubtless seen here by those who regard Hosea 6:3 as an expression of the shallow repentance of the people, who were without any conception of the seriousness of their sin.

V13: I will punish her for the days of the Baals. The word translated 'punish' often means 'to be called to account'. The judgement of God is always measured according to his strict principles of justice. The people would be called to account for their idolatry.

She decked herself. All too often false religion consists in great effort and ostentation, expressing itself in elaborate ritual (cf. *Mic.* 6:6–8).

She went after her lovers. She had sought after every device to attract these loose lovers. If men spent as much effort seeking after God as they do in the quest of lesser things, their happiness would overflow!

But Me she forgot. Apostasy has two aspects, the positive and the negative (cf. *Jer.* 2:13). People's earnest pursuit of false religion contrasts strangely with their neglect of God, although he is so kind and gracious to them. This gives ample testimony of the bondage of human minds to Satan.

The book of Deuteronomy abounds in warnings against forgetting God (4:23; 8:11, 14, 19, to note but a few). The New Testament contains a similar warning (*Heb.* 2:1–3).

FOR MEDITATION

1. Outline of chapter 2:
   a) The *pleading of God* (v1): his indictment and warning of judgement to come.
   b) The *punishment of God* (vv3–13): the complete devastation and depopulation of the land.
   c) The *promise of God* (vv14–23) to an unworthy, ungrateful and unwanted people. No one else wanted them!

2. That Israel, so greatly blessed by God, should fall away from him in such a manner is a solemn reminder of the weakness of the flesh (see *Rom.* 7:18). I can never afford to trust that wretched man, myself. My sufficiency must always be from God (*2 Cor.* 3:5) and my walk dependent upon him.

3. V2: God's threatenings are always a call to repentance. We are reminded of our responsibility to the family and the community. We are called to challenge ungodliness in a humble and caring, but steadfast way.

4. V3: *As in the day she was born.* We should continually remember our complete poverty apart from the new birth we have in Jesus Christ. We were dead in trespasses and sins but are now alive in Christ (*Eph.* 2:1–5), for which we should be full of gratitude. A letter from Thomas Goodwin to his son illustrates this:

> When I was threatening to become cold in my ministry, and when I felt that the Sabbath morning was coming, and my heart was not filled with amazement at the love of God, do you know what I used to do? I used to take a turn up and down among the sins of my past life, and I always came down again with a broken and a contrite heart, ready to preach, as it was preached in the beginning, the forgiveness of sins. I do not think that I ever went up the pulpit stair that I did not stop for a moment at the foot of it and take a turn up and down among the sins of my past years.

5. V4: *Children of harlotry.* Individuals went astray because they consented to the national apostasy. Are we, too, in danger of being enmeshed in this way? The prophetic message to Israel still applies to the church. Perhaps our main danger today is from so-called Christendom, which is so largely unresponsive to the warnings about the danger of loving the world (*1 John* 2:15–17).

6. V6: *A way hedged up.* There are divine disciplines: practically, as when the schemes of my life seem to be frustrated; spiritually, when although I seem to be prosperous and apparently the envy of all my neighbours, I am still restless and dissatisfied; and economically, when the money does not seem to go around (cf. *Hag.* 1:6). Do I earn money to put it in a bag full of holes?

7. V9: Are we enjoying the blessings of God but attributing them to our own efforts and intelligence, the beneficence of the state, the favour of men, or good luck? We need to be reminded that all things are his. We may do the husbandry and the manufacturing, but the raw material, the climatic condition, the strength and the wit by which we produce the goods are all his gift (*James* 1:17). We ought to approach life with godly fear (*James* 4:13–16) and continual gratitude (*Psa.* 103:1–5).

8. V10: *None shall deliver her.* None can; none will. Remember the story of the impotent man in John 5. Too many cry out and complain that 'there is no one' when they should be calling upon the Lord Jesus Christ, the man who was God and who alone is competent to meet the need. He can, and he cares enough to be willing. He loves the unlovely. The extent of human failure is reflected in Ezekiel 22:30, where it is said that there was no one to stand in the gap. This is transcended by the divine concern expressed in Isaiah 63:5: 'I wondered that *there was* no one to uphold; therefore My own arm brought salvation for Me.'

9. V13: *She went after her lovers.* The energies we devote to our business and our hobbies often throw into strong relief our indifference to spiritual things. We need to attend to some practical considerations:

How much time and money do I give to my comforts and hobbies, and how much to the Lord in worship and service?

Am I more diligent in my secular work than I am in the worship and service of God?

Am I more attentive to the desires of my friend or partner than I am to knowing and doing the will of God for me?

Am I more concerned to be in fashion than to be found in Christ? Do I want to be with it or with him?

10. The echoes of the Book of Deuteronomy and the anticipations of the Book of Ezekiel here should remind us of the timelessness of the Scriptures. We should be asking the Lord to speak to us now through Hosea.

11. The theme of restoration will be developed in the next section, but it should be noted here. The chastenings were calculated to bring about repentance. God is abidingly faithful to his covenant (*1 Cor.* 1:8–9). He may chasten us severely, but his intention is to bring us to repentance (*2 Sam.* 7:14–15).

12. *Celebrations.* The great festivals were intended to be times of great joy in the Lord, but the people had become so intoxicated with them that they had lost sight of the glorious, spiritual redemption the festivals were celebrating. In the midst of the pressures of our post-Christian age, may the Lord keep us from that sort of empty foolishness! May the Lord sanctify to us such seasons as Christmas and Easter, and may we watch against our regular weekly worship becoming a time of entertainment or an empty formality.

13. *She forgot.* John Newton, the converted slave trader who became one of the leaders in the evangelical wing of the Church of England, kept the text of Deuteronomy 15:15 on his mantlepiece: 'You shall remember you were a slave in the land of Egypt and the Lord your God redeemed you.' The sacrament of the Lord's Supper is ordained by God to remind us of that same

truth. The realisation that we have been bought at such a price should control our daily living and, like John Newton, we should daily remind ourselves of it.

Israel in the wilderness also had her ordinances of worship, the daily sacrifices, the Sabbaths, the ordained festivals, but she still forgot. It is not enough to have laws and regulations; we need also the inward working of the Holy Spirit that God alone can give. We must realise daily our dependence upon him and seek him for a tender heart, as in the prayer of Charles Wesley's hymn:

> *O for a heart to praise my God,*
> *A heart from sin set free,*
> *A heart that always feels the blood,*
> *So freely spilt for me.*
> *A heart resigned, submissive, meek,*
> *My Great Redeemer's throne,*
> *Where only Christ is heard to speak,*
> *And Jesus reigns alone.*

Chapter 2:14–23

Hope of Restoration

The cycle of judgement and promise continues following the pattern set in Chapter 1:2–9 and 1:10–2:1.

V14: **Allure**. Calvin has 'incline'. Some have suggested the very down-to-earth 'court', as emphasising that God's approach would be one of grace and charm. He aims to convert through the constraint of holy love, not merely by threat or naked power. When her way has been 'hedged up' by divine disciplines to bring her to her senses and to her knees, then the purpose of grace would begin to be revealed and unfolded.

I will bring her into the wilderness (NIV: 'lead'). Some suggest 'after I have taken her into the wilderness', but we must remember that the 'taking into the wilderness' was part of the purpose of grace. It was necessary in order to convince her of her wayward heart, rebellious nature and deep need, and to show her the great concern of the divine love. It was not until the prodigal son grew desperate that he thought about all the goodness he had enjoyed in his father's house. It was in the wilderness that Israel experienced the sufficiency of divine grace and learned to be a nation in order to be prepared for entrance into the promised land.

Speak comfort (NIV: 'speak tenderly'). The same phrase is used in Isaiah 40:2. The Lord's words were no longer of reproach and rebuke but of comfort, strength, and hope.

V15: **From there.** The NIV rather weakens the sense that this conveys, 'from the place of suffering and distress'. In the context it refers back naturally to the 'wilderness' of the previous verse. In Isaiah 35 we have the same thought of the Lord transforming the wilderness.

The Valley of Achor. The place of troubling becomes a door of hope. This valley, near Jericho, was the very threshold of the promised land. In Joshua 7, it was the place of the expiation of the sin of Achan and was seen as a door of hope. When the sin had been dealt with, Israel was able to triumph at Ai and then to advance into the land. Just as in those days discipline had been the herald of blessing, so now judgement would be the forerunner of grace.

Sing. Some translators have preferred 'respond', but 'sing' is very suitable here, putting one in mind of Moses' song of praise after the crossing of the Red Sea (*Exod.* 15). A thought here of a 'new exodus' is more fully developed in the prophecy of Isaiah. Some have questioned whether this has ever been completely fulfilled and say it refers to a yet-future return of the Jews to Palestine. Others see its fulfilment in the 'exodus' Jesus accomplished in Jerusalem, as spoken of by Moses and Elijah (*Luke* 9:31).

V16: **My Husband; My Master** (AV: 'Ishi'; 'Baali'). Both 'Ishi' and 'Baali' are words used for 'husband', but the ideas are completely different. The first suggests a relationship of love, affection, and honour; the second speaks of a harsh lordship.

V17: **I will take from her mouth the names of the Baals.** In the light of the new covenant revealed by the Lord (*Jer.* 31: 33–34, *Ezek.* 36:25–27), we may see here a reference to the regenerating work of God's Spirit. He will erase the memory of the Baals from their minds though they have called upon them for so long.

V18: This promise reverses the curse of Amos 5:19. The fact that the curse was so completely fulfilled would give encouragement that the promise too would have its perfect fulfilment.

The **covenant** here is much more in the nature of a command, emphasising the Lordship of Jahweh (Jehovah) over nature. Though the Baals were the Canaanite gods of nature, it is the Lord who commands the world of nature. God promises to remove all that which might hurt or harm. These blessings are linked with the new covenant in Jeremiah and Ezekiel and are found in such passages as Isaiah 11 and 35.

Earth (NIV: 'land'). Some argue that 'land' is the more suitable translation, since the prophecy is dealing mainly with Israel. Others keep the universal 'earth', the final kingdom being a universal kingdom.

V19: **Betroth.** This word applies to the wooing of a maiden, not the restoration of a wife. It may be emphasising the wonder of what is being done: there is a completely new beginning, the old things having passed away (*2 Cor.* 5:17). The former betrothal had been annulled by Israel's apostasy, but the Lord would again take the initiative, and the new relationship would be distinguished from the former one by the fact that it was for ever. Here again the new covenant is anticipated: the fear of the Lord would be implanted in such a way that the people would not again depart from him (*Jer.* 32:38–40). Isaiah 54: 5–8 uses the imagery of the restoration of the deserted wife.

Certain characteristics of this betrothal are enumerated which display the glory of the moral nature of the Lord God.

Righteousness is an essential quality of God demonstrated in the assurance of Abraham when he was interceding for Sodom: 'Shall not the Judge of all the earth do right?' (*Gen.* 18:25). However, more than moral integrity is involved in the divine righteousness, again indicated in Abraham's experience, when it is said that he believed God and he counted it to him for righteousness (*Gen.* 15:6). Salvation is through the righteousness of God.

Righteousness is the quality of the divine character that enables God to receive sinful men without compromising his character as just and holy. Paul says that God commends his love to us in that Christ died while we were still sinners (*Rom.* 5:8). He explains (*Rom.* 3:21–26) that this is not at the expense of his righteousness. God receives sinful men on the grounds of the atoning sacrifice of the Lord Jesus Christ, described there as a 'propitiation' – that which appeases wrath. The very act that expresses his wrath against sin is also the supreme expression of this forgiving love. In Old Testament times God's salvation was granted on the grounds of the sacrifice to be offered by the Lord Jesus Christ in the fullness of God's time (*Rom.* 3:25).

This righteousness is not only imputed to us on the basis of the merits of the perfect and finished work of Christ, but is also imparted to us progressively through the work of the Holy Spirit. We are born again of the Spirit and put on the new man created in righteousness and true holiness (*Eph.* 4:22–24). This is the righteousness of God through faith in Jesus Christ (*Rom.* 3:22).

Justice is defined by John Calvin as 'rectitude in which nothing is wanting'. God always deals with his creatures in perfect justice. No one can complain that his justice has been harsh.

Lovingkindness and mercy. God's love for unworthy creatures does not fail, nor his covenant mercy. Calvin comments: 'Though the people were unworthy, yet this would be no impediment in their way to prevent them returning to God, for in this reconciliation God would have regard to his own goodness rather than the merits of his people.'

V20: **Faithfulness.** This new arrangement would be fixed and unchangeable because the divine gift would guarantee for the people what they had previously lacked. God himself would establish their hearts. This truth is seen in the New Testament (*1 Pet.* 5:10).

You shall know the LORD. This personal intimacy of relationship is also indicated in Jeremiah 31:34. We may see this illustrated in the contrast between the giving of the law at Mount Sinai and the Sermon on the Mount. In the former, the people were kept at a distance, and God gave the law to Moses, the mediator, who then took it to the people. In the Sermon on the Mount, God in Jesus Christ personally gave the Word, and the people gathered at his feet to receive the Word directly. We may note that in both the knowledge of God is more than a philosophical theory; it is a living experience (*1 Thess.* 1:5–6).

V21: **I will answer.** Though translators differ somewhat, the sense is clear enough. All the required resources would be provided by God in answer to prayer (See *Isa.* 65:24, *Matt.* 7:7.).

V22: **Jezreel.** Poole here catches the sense well, speaking of 'God's seed', recalling the play on words in 1:11. God's scattering becomes God's seed. They would enjoy the privileges accorded to sons and daughters, as in the restoration of the prodigal son in the parable of Jesus (*Luke* 15:22–24).

V23 The play on the word is continued in the introduction here of sowing.

You *are* My people (1:11) is met by the wholehearted response, ***You are* my God**, as when Thomas worshipped the risen Lord (*John* 20:28).

We note again that in the New Testament these promises are applied to the church of the Lord Jesus Christ (*1 Pet.* 2:10).

FOR MEDITATION

1. Outline for 2:14–23:
   a) *God speaking tenderly* (v14): the word of grace.
   b) *Israel singing sweetly* (v15): the song of redemption.
   c) *God saving graciously* (vv19–20, 23): the promise of betrothal.

2. The Lord takes his people into the wilderness to allure them. 'Behind a frowning providence he hides a smiling face,' wrote William Cowper. The 'wilderness days' of our Christian experience can become a rich blessing as we open our hearts to the divine mercy in submission to his good and perfect will.

Two quotations from earlier writers illustrate this truth.

a) Daniel Rowland, from a sermon on Romans 8:28:

Even affliction is very useful and profitable for the godly. The prodigal son had no thought of returning to his father's house until he was humbled by adversity. Hagar was haughty under Abraham's roof and despised her mistress, but in the wilderness she was meek and lowly. Jonah sleeps on board ship, but in the whale's belly, he watches and prays. Manasseh lived as a libertine in Jerusalem and committed the most enormous crimes, but when he was bound in chains in the prison in Babylon, his heart was turned to seek the Lord his God. Bodily disease and pain have been instrumental in rousing many to seek for Christ, among those who, when in high health, have given themselves no concern about him. The ground which is not rent and torn by the plough bears nothing but thistles and thorns. The vines will run wild in the process of time if they be not pruned or trimmed. So would our wild hearts be overrun with filthy poisonous weeds if the true vinedresser did not often check their growth by crosses and sanctified troubles . . . There can be no gold or silver finely wrought without first being purified by fire, and no elegant houses can be built with stones until the hammers have squared and smoothed them. So, we can neither become vessels of honour in the house of God until we are melted in the furnace of affliction, or lively stones in the walls of the New Jerusalem till the Lord has beaten off our proud excrescences and tumours with his own hammers.[1]

b) Thomas Brooks, the Puritan writer, commenting on Hosea 2:14:

God makes afflictions to be but inlets to the soul's more sweet and full enjoyment of his blessed self. When was it Stephen saw the heavens open . . . but when the stones were about his ears? When did God appear in his glory to Jacob, but in the day of his troubles when the stones were his pillows and the ground his bed?[2]

3. How wonderfully are the divine attributes of holiness and love blended in the revelation of the divine activity. When we consider these attributes intellectually, we run into what seems a paradox. But when we see them demonstrated in the personal redeeming activity of God, the intellectual problems are transcended by the perfection of the revelation culminating at the cross, where we see wrath and mercy meeting in the propitiation (Greek: *hilasterion,* the sacrifice that turns away wrath). Here indeed, the place Achor ('troubling') becomes a door of hope.

4. The Lord speaks tenderly to his people because he is the God of all comfort. (*2 Cor.* 1:3–5). His compassions do not fail (*Lam.* 3:22–23).

---

[1] Quoted by J.C. Ryle in *Christian Leaders of the 18th Century* (Edinburgh: Banner of Truth, 1997), pp. 206–207.

[2] In *Precious Remedies against Satan's Device*s (Edinburgh: Banner of Truth, 1993), pp. 81–82.

5. Vv14–15: *Vineyards from there.* In Isaiah 35 it is promised that the desert shall rejoice and blossom as the rose. Such is the power of transforming grace. Ask: what of the wilderness places in my life? Do I desire that they be transformed? In Hosea 10:12, God has revealed that this is possible. How foolish to turn away from God and prefer a wilderness to a vineyard!

6. The *Valley of Achor*

a) There is a place of sowing in tears. Repentance and putting away of accursed things are necessary to the enjoyment of communion with God and his blessing (*Josh.* 7).

b) There is a place of the season of opportunity. The Lord creates the opportunity by bringing us to the place of tears, but the opportunity is in its very nature limited. The day of grace is *now* (*2 Cor.* 6:2). The fetters of sin strengthen continually: death stalks the prey. Only as we learn to mourn over sin can we find the peace of sin forgiven (*Matt.* 5:4). This is urgent.

c) There is a place of satisfaction at last, a door of hope in the place of disillusionment and disappointment. Like Israel, we often look in the wrong places for our bread (strength), water (life), wool (the covering garment of security), and wine (satisfaction); but Christ is the door of hope.

> *I heard the voice of Jesus say:*
> *Come unto me and rest;*
> *Behold I freely give the living water, thirsty one;*
> *I am this dark world's light.*
> *I looked to Jesus*
> *and I found in him my star, my sun!*
>
> – Horatius Bonar

Alexander Maclaren summarises these truths in a powerful sermon on Hosea 2:15:

> The valley of Achor was the place where Achan was stoned.
> Achan has to be killed and put safe out of the way first, or no

shining hope will stand out against the black walls of the defile. The taste which knits us to the perishable world, the yearnings for Babylonish garments and wedges of gold must be coerced and subdued. Swift, sharp unrelenting justice must be done on the lust of the flesh, the lust of the eye and the pride of life if our trials are ever to become doors of hope . . . so the trouble which detaches us from earth gives us new hope.[3]

7. V15: *She shall sing*. It is right that the Lord's people should express their praise in song (*Psa.* 98:1).

Songs of redemption are found in Exodus 15, Isaiah 12:1–5 and Revelation 5:5–9. See also Exodus 15:2, Psalm 118:14, and Isaiah 12:2: the Lord is my strength, song, and salvation.

The situation was one of extreme danger.
The salvation was solely by the grace of God.
The song of praise is to so great a redeemer.

The Lord's people are intended to be a 'singing people' (*Eph.* 5:19, *Col.* 3:16).

8. *Ishi* or *Baali*? In the long run I cannot manage without a lord. But who is my lord, Christ or Satan? Christ, full of grace and truth, to whom we become espoused in love? Or Satan, the god of this world, to whom we would remain slaves for ever, but for almighty grace? Grace brings a complete change of allegiance. How deep is my commitment to the Lord Jesus Christ?

9. V18: *Lie down in safety*. The promise is illustrated in Psalm 23 and perfectly realised in the words of Jesus (*John* 10:9–10). As Paul puts it, He is our peace (*Eph.* 2:14).

---

[3] In *The Books of Ezekiel, Daniel and the Minor Prophets* (London: Hodder & Stoughton, 1908), p.96.

The storm may roar without me
My heart may low be laid,
But God is round about me,
And can I be dismayed?

Anna Laetitia Waring

10. Vv 19–20: Through the wonder of the new covenant, the Lord makes each one of us a new creation (*2 Cor.* 5:17) in respect of:

a) Our standing before God. We are justified (*Rom.* 5:1);

b) Our affections. We are sanctified (*Phil.* 3:10–11);

c) Our satisfaction in living. We are content (*Phil.* 4:11–13).

11. This passage from the Puritan John Flavel can help us meditate on the wonder of the divine love, especially as we remember that it comes from one of those who were famed for their sobriety and carefulness of language:

> It is a special consideration to enhance the love of God in giving Christ, that in giving him, he gave the richest jewel in his cabinet, a mercy of the greatest worth and the most inestimable value. Heaven itself is not so valuable as Christ is. He is the better half of heaven; and so the saints account him (*Psa.* 73:25). Ten thousand thousand worlds, as many worlds as angels can number, and then as a new world of angels can multiply, would not be all the bulk of a balance to weigh Christ's excellency, love and sweetness. Oh, what a fair One, what an only One, what an excellent, lovely, ravishing One is Christ. Put the beauty of ten thousand paradises, like the Garden of Eden into one . . . Oh, what a fair and excellent thing that would be! And yet it should be less to that fair, dearest and well-beloved Christ, than one drop of rain to the whole seas, rivers, lakes, and fountains of ten thousand earths. Christ is heaven's wonder and earth's wonder.

Now, for God to bestow the mercy of mercies, the most precious thing in heaven and earth upon poor sinners: and as great, as lovely, as excellent as his Son was, yet not to account him too good to bestow upon us, what manner of love is this![4]

12. The final verses of the chapter should cause the Christian to think of the glorified world yet to come, anticipated in Romans 8:19–23 and pictured in Revelation 21–22. We shall be not angels floating around in space, but inhabitants of the new glorified world freed from the curse. Here is the hope and encouragement of all who are in Christ (*1 John* 3:1–3). If the whole of creation is waiting eagerly for this, how much more should the believer be inspired to eager longing by his eternal hope?

---

[4] In *The Works of John Flavel, Vol. 1* (Edinburgh: Banner of Truth, 1997), pp.67–68.

Chapter 3:1–5

The Patience of Restoring Love

The story of the prophet's domestic life with Gomer is taken up again.

V1: The work of restoration follows because God has directed him to it. The demonstration of compassion expresses not just the heart of the prophet, but the heart of God.

Loved by a lover. Scholars debate the exact meaning of this. Many suggest that it means 'in love with a paramour', but Calvin, Poole and Keil all agree that the word means 'husband' (cf. *Jer.* 3:20, *Song of Sol.* 5:16). The first emphasises the way-wardness of her affections, the other, the steadfastness of the husband's love. Both suit the context.

The command is not merely to pity, but to love as God loves and to seek to save her from herself. True, there is pity, but it is a pity born of the steadfast faithfulness of the covenant love of God. It is not a little humanitarian aid, but a commitment to restoration with transformation. God will seek his Israel, though they have completely estranged themselves.

Raisin cakes is probably better than the AV 'flagons of wine', since these raisin cakes were associated with the Baal festivals in which Israel took great pleasure at this time. Perhaps the general thought is of the nation's delight in sensual pleasures.

V2: The redemption price was apparently half the price of a slave (*Exod.* 21:32) and grain enough to provide a meagre one-day ration. This evidently illustrated the depths to which Gomer, and the nation, had fallen. She was, as it were, on the cut-price counter, with her shame exposed for all to see. The divine love is here expressed not in the price paid, but in the shame and worthlessness of the one being redeemed.

V3: Some understand the verse to indicate a wife so moved by the love of her husband that the desire to stray has gone: the husband's love and faithfulness have triumphed at last. Others see a wife under discipline: 'You shall stay with me many days'. The final part of the verse ('so, too, *will* I *be* toward you') indicates that Hosea will share the trials of her rehabilitation in a spirit of loyal sacrifice, for the present denying himself a husband's right.

V4: The application to the children of Israel is made, indicating a period of discipline in which Israel would be deprived of her national and spiritual institutions, both false and true. During the Babylonian captivity, Israel did forsake idol worship but did not enjoy real intimacy with the Lord. This verse, however, probably refers primarily to the Northern Kingdom, which was scattered around the Assyrian empire and seems to have been lost. Even today the nation does not enjoy the intimacy of fellowship with the Lord that comes from the knowledge of Jesus as the Messiah, since they continue in rejection of him.

Scholars do not agree as to whether this refers to all religious institutions, both false and true, or whether in this case all are wholly false. It is doubtful whether any of the religious institutions of the Northern Kingdom can be regarded as true, though perhaps some individuals were faithful to the Lord.

Without king. The Northern Kingdom was, in a sense, an act of apostasy from the beginning.

Sacrifice. In the north, the sacrifices were made to images representing the Lord. The whole religious culture was therefore astray, since the law forbade any form of idolatry. Moreover, they were offered at sanctuaries not appointed by God, and by priests not approved by him.

Sacred pillar. These were the images representing the Baals and their consorts.

Ephod. Exactly what is referred to here is in doubt. It may refer to some kind of cultic symbol, or to some part of the priestly clothing (see *Judg.* 8:24–28).

Teraphim. These were the household images (see *Gen.* 31:19; 30–35). Jacob, in his re-consecration at Bethel, ordered his household to put these away (*Gen.* 35:2). Some scholars have argued that these were permitted before the Exile, but that is scarcely likely in view of both Jacob's action and the clear teaching of the law of Moses. The fact that they are mentioned in the Old Testament does not mean that they were ever legal, but rather, indicates the extent to which the nation had gone astray from God. Speculations as to their legality are based on the supposition that Israel's religion evolved out of its surroundings, a view not justified from the teaching of the Old Testament itself.

The combination reflected here shows how Israel had mingled the true and the false, much of it culled from the surrounding heathen nations, demonstrating their utter failure to realise the divine intention that they should be a separated people (*Exod.* 19:5–6).

V5: The brief chapter concludes with a promise of restoration, which must be Messianic in character.

Afterwards [they] shall return. Calvin remarks that they are now led away headlong into their impiety, and they can by no means be restrained, except by this long endurance of evils. Restoration can come about only by repentance, yet it is wholly by God's initiative. This is no 'if' and 'but' promise, but a definite statement that the mighty working of divine grace will eventually bring them to repentance. The change of heart proves that God is at work. He commands men to repent, and their response is the evidence of his effectual call. Men are hopeless except as he works in mercy.

The LORD their God. The name of the Lord is set in contrast to the others to whom they had been offering allegiance as gods.

David their king. God had promised that the line of David would endure (*2 Sam.* 7:16; 23:5, *Psa.* 72:5, 17). God's word to Hosea here looks forward to the fulfilment of this older prophecy. The Northern Kingdom is warned that there can be no restoration apart from their reconciliation to the house of David, which will come about through the person of the Messiah. Calvin writes on this verse: 'God is not to be sought, except in Christ the Mediator. Whoever forsakes Christ forsakes God himself, for as John says, he who has not the Son, has not the Father' (*1 John* 2:23). Some expositors argue that only one person is intended here, that is, the Lord their God in the person of David their king, though they would not argue that the prophet would be fully aware of this. 1 Peter 1:10–12 makes clear that the prophets did not always understand the full implications of their message, but knew that it applied to a future time when the Messiah would be revealed.

They shall fear the LORD and His goodness. The goodness of God, as revealed in his saving grace, creates in the believer an attitude of reverential fear (*Psa.* 130:3–4). Calvin remarks that the goodness of God here refers to Christ, 'since it is so exhibited in him that not a particle is to be sought anywhere else'.

In the latter days. In the thinking of the prophets, this referred to the time when God would establish his everlasting kingdom in the person of the Messiah (*Isa.* 2:2, *Joel* 2:28–32 with *Acts* 2:17; *Mic.* 4:1, *Heb.* 1:2). The end of all things is not confusion, but the kingdom!

FOR MEDITATION

1. Outline for the chapter:
   a) The *representation of the divine love.*
   b) The *redemption of the unfaithful wife.*
   c) The *requirement of a disciplined life.*
   d) The *response of the awakened people.*
   e) The *richness of the divine blessing.*

2. Dwell on the triumph of the divine love. God will not let his people go. The gracious, though sometimes severe, hand of his providence and the constraint of his Spirit will work to restore the wayward believer. Whom he loves he chastens (*Heb.* 12:6). Each person is a responsible agent: God will not save us in our sin, only out of it. The evidence of the presence of grace is in our forsaking of sin. There is no easy assurance. We must each examine ourselves as to whether we are truly in Christ (*2 Cor.* 13:5), and then give diligence to make our calling and election sure (*2 Pet.* 1:10). Though there is never any doubt of this in the mind of God, there may be doubt in us, in our understanding of it, and in its demonstration in our manner of life. 1 John 2:1–6 states the evidences clearly and briefly. Doubts and subnormal Christian living are not to be dealt with by the doling out of superficial comfort, crying peace where there is no peace, as did the false prophets in Jeremiah's day (*Jer.* 6:14). Neither are we to seek some shallow emotional experience of instant salvation, but to commit ourselves to dependence on the inward work of the Spirit of God through the regular application of his Word. The salvation of God is worked in us by his grace and worked out by us in daily life (*Phil.* 2:12–13).

3. V2: People are rarely prepared to accept their true position in the sight of God as slaves of sin (*Rom.* 6:17). Hosea could recover his wife cheaply enough, but God in his holiness must

pay the ransom by the death of his Son (*Acts* 20:28). The price God has paid for us at the cross is one of the wonders of grace. The price reflects not our worth, but the greatness of his love and the awfulness of our sin in the sight of God.

4. V5: David as king represents the rule of God and true worship. We cannot worship God except through King Jesus. We must continually ask ourselves if he is truly the king of our lives. It is not enough to have him as a constitutional monarch, with self as the prime minister! He does not offer himself on terms (*Luke* 9:57–62; 14:26–27; 18:22).

5. The compromised state of Israel's religion is mirrored in much of what passes for Christianity today, where the very clear teaching of Scripture is set aside to appear modern and win favour with people in the world. Such issues as wide ranging as the priesthood, the ordination of women, homosexuality, euthanasia, abortion and evangelistic methods all need to be examined in the light of the teaching of Scripture. There is great need for clear teaching on the final authority of the Scriptures as the infallible Word of God and on the person and work of the Lord Jesus Christ. His deity, the atonement, resurrection and ascension, the final judgement and Christ's return in glory are all much neglected truths. We need to return to the truth that salvation is by grace through faith alone. How much of what the churches teach is determined by Scripture, and how much by the spirit of the age?

2 Timothy 3:16–17 states clearly the authority and the sufficiency of Scripture.

Chapter 4:1–14

The Controversy of God with His People

Verse 1: Compare with 2:2. The prophets often use the language of the courtroom (cf. *Isa.* 43:9–10). God has a complaint against his people in that they have failed to fulfil their covenant responsibilities to show truth, mercy, and knowledge of God. Salvation is expressed in life. We are reminded that the godly life is not the cause but the consequence of God's saving grace (cf. 2:19–20).

Truth; mercy; knowledge of God. Compare this with God's promise in 2:19.

Truth. This involves integrity in government and abiding constancy of loyalty and purpose in personal life. It means faithfulness (*Psa.* 15:2).

Mercy. The Hebrew (*hesed*) is frequently used of the covenant faithfulness of God, but is also found to describe human relationships showing gentleness and compassion towards those in need, thus reflecting the nature of God's dealings with his people.

The word is used by Abraham's servant when requesting the Lord's favour in leading him to a bride for Isaac (*Gen.* 24.12). It is used of God's mercy to Joseph in prison (*Gen.* 39:21). Rahab uses it in her request for 'kindness' in response to her 'kindness' to the spies.

In the New Testament the same idea is seen in the requirement to forgive as we have been forgiven (*Eph.* 4:32, *Col.* 3:13).

Knowledge refers to the relationship with God which expresses itself in the fulfilment of his moral requirements.

V6 makes clear that the failure of Israel in this respect was deliberate and wilful.

Vv 2–3: The list of the virtues they lacked is followed by a list of the vices they practised.

Swearing. The blasphemous use of the Lord's name indicates a lack of respect for him, and often an unbridled desire to call down evil upon others. It displays a rebellious and godless heart.

Lying refers to all speaking and practising falsehood and denying the truth.

Killing refers to all kinds of civic violence: murder, blood feuds, bloodshed, and even bringing death upon others by heartless oppression (*Amos* 4:1–4 and *Mic.* 6:10–12 deal with the same kind of evil).

Stealing may be accomplished by false weights and measures as well as by actual pillaging of the property of others.

Committing adultery. Sexual immorality was a continual problem in this society, for wherever the Baal worship existed the fertility rites encouraged cultic prostitution and led to license in the society as a whole.

Contrast this with the strictness of the law of Moses in these matters. The teaching of Jesus on divorce reflects the strictness of the law revealed at Sinai (*Matt.* 19:3–9). The sanctity of marriage is an important principle in Scripture (*Matt.* 19:4–6).

They break all restraint. Here we have a permissive society in which the law of God is flouted, the restraints of social conscience defied and the individual conscience seared.

Bloodshed. Violence abounded and life was counted cheap. The rule of law had broken down.

V3: **Therefore.** Sin has its inevitable consequence: it will bring inescapable disaster (*Num.* 32:23).

The land will mourn. Those who seek self-fulfilment in defiance of the laws of God will be brought to sorrow. The fruitfulness of the land itself will be affected. The land will be devastated by war, pestilence, depopulation and captivity. These are all seen as judgements from God.

This cause and effect is seen in the curse (*Gen.* 3:17–18) and reflected in the promise of restoration (*Rom.* 8:20–22). Here is a warning which the modern world would do well to heed. Where the restraints of the divine order are broken and materialism holds sway, ecological problems will result.

V4: Various interpretations have been suggested for this verse:

a) Great though their sin is, it is pointless to rebuke it, since they are so deliberately given over to sin. Amos 8:11 speaks of a famine of the Word, and Hosea is here saying virtually the same thing. No one, not even a prophet, is to strive with the nation because the truth is to be taken from them. Even those who are true are to remain silent.

b) Do not spend time in mutual recrimination, since the Lord's contention is with the priests, who should have been the watchmen in the nation, and the shepherds, guarding its moral integrity. God will call them to account first of all.

c) Calvin and Poole agree that the verse means that all have sinned to such a degree that none is in a position to rebuke another. They are like those who strive with the priest: they show no reverence or respect, boasting that their knowledge is superior to that of their teachers and wilfully opposing sound doctrine. God had intended that the priest should be the final authority in matters of law (*Deut.* 17:12–13). 'Those who contend with the priest' may be an ancient way of branding the anarchist!

d) Michael Eaton reads a different set of vowel points, to give the sense that God's contention is with the priests.

V5: **You** most naturally refers to the priests, who along with the prophets were supposedly the religious leaders of the nation.

Stumble is probably a rather weak translation. The AV has 'fall'. The prophet and priest are singled out as those responsible for the moral and spiritual life of the nation.

In the day refers to the time when normally people would walk in safety. The thought is of their inescapable doom.

Mother usually refers to the nation, but here could mean the tribe of Levi, to which the priests belonged.

V6: The thought here is of the wilfulness of their sin.

I will reject you. This may refer particularly to the priesthood, but it could refer to the nation as a whole, since they were called by God to be a priestly nation (*Exod.* 19:6). Calvin mentions both views as possible.

Forgotten. Their forgetfulness was deliberate: they had put God's law out of mind.

Your children. The nation as a whole is doubtless in view here, but the Scriptures give frequent warnings about the effect of sin upon children (*Deut.* 6:5). The Old Testament has much to say about corporate responsibility, and in our highly individualistic society we need to be reminded of this as a fact of life.

a) Our behaviour affects our children.

b) We, together with our children, are greatly affected by the society of which we are a part.

c) We, in our turn, greatly affect the society of which we are a part. We cannot opt out by silence, still less by indifference. Jesus spoke of his disciples as being lights in the world (*Matt.* 5:16; cf. *Phil.* 2:15).

V7: The more they prospered, the more they sinned against God. Prosperity led them into presumption, against which the Lord through Moses had warned (*Deut.* 8:11–14.)

I will change their glory into shame. The traditional Jewish reading is, 'They have changed my glory into shame', and it is suggested that this refers to idolatry. Baal was on occasion called Baal Bosheth, the 'shame of Israel' (see 9:10). Either reading gives excellent sense. They had exchanged the glory of God for the idols. Equally, God would change their glory, their prosperity and their status as his chosen people, when he took them away, shattered captives, into exile. The land flowing with milk and honey would be changed into a desolate wasteland.

V8: **They** probably refers to the priests, greedily eating up the offerings brought by the people. The more the people sinned, the more offerings they must bring, and the more the priests had to eat. The situation was not unlike that with the sons of Eli, when Samuel was young (*1 Sam.* 2:13–17). There have always been some ready to profit personally from their position in the religious establishment!

V9: People and priests were alike in their sin. It is interesting that here the people are mentioned first. Although the priests were the leaders of the people and were setting them a bad example, the people were getting the priests they deserved and were fully responsible.

Reward here suggests a proportion between doings and consequences ('the wages of sin', *Rom.* 6:23).

V10 shows the dissatisfaction of their rebellious walk. The same thought is expressed in Haggai 1:6. Though the sin was more sophisticated and less blatant in Haggai's time, the fundamental evil was the same. God was not being put in his rightful place at the centre, either in national or in private life.

They shall commit harlotry and not increase. The absolute sovereign power of God as the Lord and giver of life is here demonstrated. It is likely that this refers to the fertility rites connected with the Asherah, the female consorts of the Baals. Calvin comments: 'However much they give rein to their promiscuous lusts, I will not yet suffer them to propagate. The prophet here testifies, in a word, that the ungodly are deceived when they think that they can attain their wishes by illicit and unlawful means, for the Lord will frustrate their desires.'

Because. The reason for their failure and frustration was that they had turned away from God. In their case, they were enslaved by lust. But turning away from God can also be done respectably in the eyes of the world. The essence of sin is turning to one's own way (*Isa.* 53:6), and some ways of doing this are highly sophisticated, even religious.

V11: Their uncontrolled self-indulgence had seduced them from their loyalty to God and made them slaves. The combination of the two words for 'wine' suggests drunkenness.

V12: **Wooden *idols*.** There is no noun in the Hebrew, and the reference may be particularly to the Asherah poles.

Staff may refer to the practice of rhabdomancy, the occult use of divining sticks to obtain guidance. (Ezekiel 21:21 may refer to this practice by the king of Babylon.) The language expresses scorn at such folly (cf. *Isa.* 44:15–17).

The spirit of harlotry indicates a heart enslaved by and addicted to immorality and idolatry.

V13 continues the description of the various heathen rites practised by the people.

Mountaintops. The name 'high places' was literally true, as mountaintops and other prominent points were used as centres of worship, possibly because they were thought to bring the worshippers closer to the heavenly bodies they worshipped.

Burn incense. One of the marks of heathen worship was its elaborate ritual.

Oaks, poplars and terebinths refer to the high and lofty trees found at many of these centres of worship. It is mentioned here that their shade is good. This may indicate either that the practices indulged in at these places was not fit for the light of day, or it may indicate concern for creature comforts. Self-indulgence was a mark of most pagan worship.

Daughters; brides. This reference reveals that the worship of the Asherah was thoroughly degrading to women. Astarte, represented by the Asherah poles, was the Phoenician goddess of love. It is in the worship of God alone that we have a true concept of love in its tenderness, faithfulness, and self-sacrifice. It should be noted that the loss of awareness of God is the reason for the tawdriness of what passes for love in much modern literature, in television, and in human behaviour.

V14: Some suggest that this should be read as a question, expecting the answer 'yes'. In this case the prophet is appealing to the people, assuming that, in the light of what they know of their sins and the nature of God, they must, if there is an iota of truth left in them, pass judgement upon their sins. Michael Eaton suggests that the Hebrew *lo* should be read *lu*, replacing the negative with 'surely'. But the reading given in NIV and NKJ, 'I will not punish', can be defended. Calvin understands the meaning to be: '"I will not correct them for their scandalous behaviour, for I wish them to be exposed to infamy." When men are wilfully determined to be blind, it is no wonder that the Lord gives them up.' Because of their sinfulness, they will not be corrected as though they were children of the covenant.

For *the men* themselves. The men should have been setting a better example, but they were indulging in ritual prostitution.

The final phrase makes clear that at last this rebellious nation would be brought to ruin.

FOR MEDITATION

1. Outline for chapter 4:
   a) The *state of the nation* (vv1–3).
   b) The *stumbling block of the priesthood* (vv4–10).
   c) The *sins of misguided people* (vv11–14).
   d) The *separation commanded* (vv15–19).

2. The Lord's judgement: read 2 Corinthians 5:10. Christ's words about disciples, servants and stewards (*Matt.* 25:14–30, *Luke* 12: 31–48; 19:11–26) remind us that God's people are accountable and that the highest standards are expected at all times. Romans 14:12 also confirms that an accounting is to be rendered. When we have thought this through we shall doubtless feel our great need for the glorious promises like those in Isaiah 1:18, Matthew 11:28, and 1 John 1:9.

3. The sins listed in verse 2 are those of a permissive society, which some would try to tell us represent man grown to adulthood. Hosea indicates that these sins represent man close to final reprobation. With this we may compare Romans 1:18–32. This is the verdict of the judge of all.

4. When men turn away from God, all kinds of cruelties follow. Because of our sinful nature we need the restraints of the law. Not for a moment can the Christian suggest that salvation is obtained by the keeping of the law (*Gal.* 3:10–11), but we need it nonetheless. It is by the law we come to understand what sin is (*Rom.* 3:20), and by the law behaviour may be restrained. The law of God applied to the conscience by the Holy Spirit causes us to see our moral bankruptcy and need of the salvation which God has provided in and through the Lord Jesus Christ (*Rom.* 7:7–25). We must never forget that the law is holy and good, and it cannot be cast aside like an old worn-out shoe. It declares the intention of God for moral behaviour.

The Holy Spirit uses it to bring conviction of sin and then brings our hearts to obey in a spirit of grateful love.

5. We need to be reminded of the special responsibility of the prophet and priest. It applies to ministry today, when churches can be somewhat careless about what is taught or who governs, teaches, or occupies the pulpit. Some are flattered to be given such offices, but the Scriptures warn of the special responsibility before God in such matters (*Ezek*. 18, *James* 3:1). We should not covet leadership, but neither dare we shirk it, should the call come to us. The call to minister God's Word should not be lightly undertaken. Listen to Hugh Latimer, preaching before Henry VIII, that monarch of uncertain temper and even more uncertain sympathy to the doctrines of the Reformation:

> I must show forth such things as I have learned in Scripture or else deny Jesus Christ, the denying of which ought to be more dreaded than the loss of all temporal goods, honour . . . and the fear of all manner of torments and cruelties, yea and death itself, be it never so shameful and painful . . . As you are a mortal man, having in you the corrupt nature of Adam, so you have no less need of the merits of Christ's passion for your salvation, than I and others of your subjects have . . . Wherefore, Gracious King, remember yourself. Have pity on your soul, and think that the day is at hand when you shall give account of your office, in the which day, Your Grace may stand steadfastly and not be ashamed, but be clear and steady in your reckoning, and to have your 'quietus est' sealed with the blood of our Saviour, Jesus Christ, which only serveth at that day. This is my daily prayer to him that suffered for our sins, who also prayeth to his Father for grace for us continually.[1]

---

[1] In 'A letter to the King for restoring again the free liberty of reading the Holy Scriptures' in Vol.20, *The Works of Hugh Latimer (Sometime Bishop of Worcester)* (Cambridge: Parker Society Publications, 1845), pp.298–299, 308–309.

Bishop Ryle, commenting on his courage and faithfulness as a minister, quotes Latimer as saying in one of his sermons before the king: 'Latimer, Latimer, thou art going to speak before the high and mighty King Henry VIII, who is able, if he think fit, to take thy life away. Be careful what thou sayest. But Latimer, Latimer, remember also thou art about to speak before the King of kings and Lord of lords. Take heed thou doest not displease him.'[2]

God has no contentions with such an ambassador: may he give us grace to be such witnesses.

6. V6: the possibility of rejected knowledge. Anyone who is in the position to have knowledge but refuses it is in a place of special accountability. In Great Britain we have freedom to know and uphold the Christian gospel; the Scriptures are easily available in our language and in readable versions; in many places the gospel is still faithfully preached; and there is an abundance of Christian literature. In view of these things, ignorance of the Christian gospel is a wilful rejection of knowledge.

Unfortunately, many call themselves Christians but have little appetite for the Word of God and prefer entertainment to spiritual worship. Do we personally match up to the requirement of Colossians 3:16?

7. V12: The Scriptures point out how foolish it is to worship sticks and stones. Yet is not the materialist, however intelligent, doing just this? Is not humanism also a subtle form of idolatry with man in the place of God? There is also a danger in democracy, if the will of the people pays no respect to the will of God. In Communism and every other form of totalitarianism the state usurps the place of God. Even technology can become idolatrous. Truly there is no new thing under the sun (*Eccles.* 2:9). Modern man with all his sophistication worships gods as foolish

---

[2] J.C. Ryle, *Five English Reformers* (Edinburgh: Banner of Truth, 1999) p.106.

and illogical as the Baals and the Ashtaroths, because, although ingenious, they too are man-made. It is worth noting the recent revival of interest in astrology and the occult as some have rebelled against the dictatorship of human reason.

8. V13: The old pagan religions paid much attention to creature comforts and encouraged self-indulgence. At the very centre of the Christian gospel is the cross and the call to discipleship, which involves taking up the cross and humbling and denying self. This is on a collision course with most modern outlook, and we must ask ourselves whether our behaviour is truly Christ centred. We cannot serve God and mammon (*Matt.* 6:24). The world around us, perhaps unconsciously, has embraced much of the culture of ancient paganism, and we, like the Jews of Hosea's day, are under pressure to compromise and even conform to its lust for self-fulfilment. Solomon reminds us: 'Keep your heart with all diligence, for out of it *spring* the issues of life' (*Prov.* 4:23).

9. V14: the responsibility of the male. All too frequently men have sought to exploit some imaginary superiority of their sex and quoted the Bible in their defence. They have ignored what is actually taught in Scripture about the responsibility of the headship of the man. The woman is not there for man's use and exploitation, but to be loved, protected and guided by him. Marriage is spoken of as the earthly counterpart of the relationship between Christ and his church (*Eph.* 5:22–33). The authority of the husband is one of love and caring responsibility for the spiritual and material welfare of his wife. In this passage in Hosea, it may be argued that the responsibility of the women is lessened by the failures of the men, who have set an example in sin. Womanhood, which should have been cherished, had been debased by lust. Modern male chauvinism and feminism equally strike at the heart of the divine order. It

is in the Christian home that the pattern of godliness should be revealed, as light shining in the world, in the midst of a crooked and perverse generation (*Phil.* 2:15).

10. V14: *They will be trampled.* In history God reveals and demonstrates his moral nature and his lordship. His mercy and forbearance are seen when immediate judgement does not come upon evil men. But we do often see wickedness brought to account by disasters or by the reprobation spoken of in Romans 1:18ff. The decline and fall of the great empires of Egypt, Assyria, Babylon, Persia, Greece and Rome may be understood in this light. Each of these great empires was without faith in the true God and became corrupt. Here we see it in the scattering of Israel, which followed soon after Hosea's solemn warnings. The grace and forbearance of God was seen in his choice of Israel and his great patience with them in their rebellions (*Neh.* 9:16–19, 27–28, 30–31). But it is supremely seen in the revelation we have in the Lord Jesus Christ. His incarnation, life, death, resurrection and ascension are not mythological symbols but facts, the solid realities of the Word made flesh and dwelling among us. Believers can be confident of meeting him because he is the Lord of history.

Chapter 4:15–19

The Lord's Warning to Judah

The sad plight of Israel and its impending doom are used as a solemn warning to Judah to watch itself lest it fall into the same condemnation. The indictment of Israel continues in the strongest possible terms.

V15: Israel is condemned yet again for playing the prostitute.

Gilgal was once a place of hallowed associations. It was the place of rededication after the crossing of the Jordan (*Josh.* 5:9). It symbolised the completion of the great journey called the Exodus, for it was here that Israel truly entered the land. It was the base for Joshua's campaign of conquest, thus becoming the token of past mercies and the hope of future victories under the guidance of God. In later days, after Joshua's death, the angel of the Lord went up in judgement from Gilgal to Bochim to call to account the nation's apostasy from God (*Judg.* 2:1). The kingship of Saul was confirmed at Gilgal (*1 Sam.* 11:15).

It was also here that Saul offered the presumptuous and precipitate sacrifice which demonstrated the declension of his heart from the Lord (*1 Sam.* 13:7–10). It might be argued that from this time Gilgal became the symbol of the nation's rebellion against the divine rule, though it should not be forgotten that at Gilgal the nation welcomed David back as king after the abortive rebellion of Absalom (*2 Sam.* 19:15). In the eighth century it was a centre, along with Bethel, of the unspiritual worship so strongly condemned by Amos and Hosea. This shrine, once sacred to the name of the Lord, typified the nation's apostasy (*Amos* 4:4; 5:5).

Beth Aven, meaning 'house of vanity', is a play on the name *Bethel*, 'house of God', where the Lord had first appeared to Jacob (*Gen.* 28). This revered patriarchal shrine had been turned into a centre of idolatry at the institution of the Northern Kingdom by Jeroboam I (*1 Kings* 12:25–13:10).

Both places had played a part in the histories of Elijah and Elisha; there had been a school of prophets at Bethel (*2 Kings* 2:3) and at Gilgal (*2 Kings* 4:38).

Nor swear an oath. Oaths had been valid and ordained by God (*Deut.* 6:13) but were useless and even blasphemous in the context of the shrines now defiled by pagan worship.

V16: The picture of the stubborn heifer is of one that had grown lusty and strong by reason of its owner's care, but now refused to serve and do appointed duties.

Let them forage like a lamb. Calvin interprets: 'I will take them and make them like lambs; and when scattered, they will fear as in a wilderness, for there will be no flock to which they can come.' They are vulnerable among those who have taken them captive. The NIV treats this as a question: 'How then can the LORD pasture them as lambs in a meadow?' Their rebellious spirit makes it so that the Lord cannot show his love to them as their shepherd.

V17: The heart of the Northern Kingdom is wedded to idolatry. This is the relationship the people have chosen for themselves and to which they hold fast.

Let him alone. Two meanings have been suggested:

a) Israel, being reprobate, is to be left in her sin. Let the people reap the fruit of their own perverse choice.

b) Judah is warned against any compromising links with a nation so far gone into idolatry.

V18: **Their drink is rebellion.** The Hebrew is uncertain, as is shown by the variety of suggested translations; but the sense is clear enough. Calvin says, 'The prophet alludes to beastly and shameful excesses.' It may be that the linking of drunkenness and prostitution indicates a reference to the feasts held in the honour of Astarte (Ashtaroth).

The last part of the verse also presents difficulty to translators: **Rulers** is literally 'shields', here understood metaphorically.

Some translators take the phrase to mean 'they love shame more than glory' (referring back to 4:7). Calvin argues that the passage condemns the covetousness of the rulers who paid no respect to right or wrong. A Jewish tradition, noted in NKJV, supports this idea with the translation, 'her rulers shamefully love "Give".' NIV has 'their rulers dearly love shameful ways'; and NKJV, 'her rulers dearly love dishonor'.

V19: This symbolises the sudden and violent nature of Israel's downfall: she will be swept away as by the violence of a mighty wind. Her false worship will at last bring her shame, a play on 'Baal-Bosheth', the Baal who is 'shame'.

FOR MEDITATION

1. Outline for 4:15–19
   a) A *warning to Judah*.
   b) A *witness to Israel*.
   c) A *whirlwind of judgement*.

2. The recurrent note of judgement here should remind us that 'our God *is* a consuming fire' (*Heb.* 12:29). We are also reminded that the human heart is inclined to presumption because of the forbearance of God (*Eccles.* 8:11, *Rom.* 2:4–5). Romans 2 emphasises that the goodness of God leads us to repentance but also that a strictly impartial judgement at last will allow no

respect of persons. The only way we can face the judgement is through Christ, who at the cross took the judgement upon himself, being made to be sin for us (*2 Cor.* 5:21). It is for us to plead guilty and to trust ourselves to God's grace in the provision of an acceptable substitute.

3. The debasing of the sanctuaries at Bethel and Gilgal is surely a warning against the dangers of institutional religion. The house of God can become a place where false religion is propagated. In Christendom many holy places have become centres of pageant and tourism, and churches have become places where the truth of Christ is contradicted and his standards lowered or ignored. We need to watch lest our churches and denominations become vanities like the church at Sardis, which had a name that it lived but in fact was spiritually dead (*Rev.* 3:1).

4. V16: *the stubborn calf.* The tendency of the human heart is to be ungrateful. We must guard against this by:

a) realising our tendency to ingratitude and rebellion;

b) recognising the claims of God upon us as trophies of his grace;

c) reviewing continually the mercies of God;

d) repenting of the things in which we have gone astray.

The Holy Spirit will apply these lessons to our hearts as we diligently study the Scriptures.

5. V17: *Let him alone.*

a) In this age of ecumenical thinking we must not ignore the warnings of Scripture against unequal yoking (*2 Cor.* 6:14). The fact that it is difficult to work through in our contemporary society does not mean that we can afford to discount it. The counsels of the Spirit of love can never run contrary to the teaching of the Word of God. We do the cause of God no service when we compromise his truth and involve ourselves with those who deny it (see *1 John* 2:19; 4:1–6). At the same time, we must be careful to do all we can to promote the visible unity of the body of Christ, as Paul demonstrates in Romans 14.

b) If the verse is understood to refer to reprobation, two applications can be made. First, we should not be too quick to abandon those who seem to be reprobate, in our prayers for them and attempts to reach them. Second, there are scriptural warnings against this danger (e.g. *Heb.* 10:26). If these fill us with fear, let us be quick to cast ourselves upon God, that we do not fall into the snare of the devil (*1 Tim.* 3:7). It is Satan's delight, as Calvin remarked, to drive saints to madness by despair.

Turn at once to Jesus, accept his invitation, 'Come to Me, all you who labor and are heavy laden' (*Matt.*11:28). 'He is able to keep you from stumbling' (*Jude* 24).

6. Thomas Brooks on v17 and Psalm 81:12:

> A soul given up to sin is ripe for hell, a soul posting [hastening] to destruction. Ah, Lord, this mercy I humbly beg, that whatever thou dost give me up to, thou wilt not give me up to the ways of my own heart. If thou wilt give me up to be afflicted or tempted, I will patiently sit down and say, 'It is the Lord, let him do to me what seemeth good in his eyes.'[1]

7. Prayer of John Calvin on this section:

> Grant Almighty God, that since thou hast at this time, in thy mercy, deigned to gather us into thy church, and to enclose us in the boundaries of thy Word, by which thou preservest us in the true and right worship of thy majesty, – O grant that we may continue contented in this obedience to thee: and though Satan may, in many ways, attempt to draw us here and there, and we be also ourselves, by nature, inclined to evil, O grant,

[1] In *Precious Remedies against Satan's Devices*, pp.50–51.

that being confirmed in faith and united to thee by that sacred bond, we may yet constantly abide under the guidance of thy Word, and thus cleave to Christ, thy only-begotten Son, who has joined us for ever to himself, that we may never by any means turn aside from thee, but be, on the contrary, confirmed in the faith of his gospel, until at length he will receive us all in to his kingdom. Amen.

Chapter 5:1–9

Proud Israel Is Defiled

The first part of this chapter takes up again the responsibility of the priests and rulers as the leaders of the people. The principle is similar to that expounded in Ezekiel 3:16–22. If the watchman does not sound the warning, then the sinners will die in their sin, but their blood will be required at the watchman's hand. So here, if the appointed shepherds lead the people astray, they will be lost, but their blood will be required at the shepherds' hands. Though it is the the leaders who are challenged, however, the nation herself has a clear responsibility before God.

V1: **Mizpah** means 'watchtower'. It was the place where Samuel had led the people in spiritual renewal (*1 Sam.* 7:2–12) and to a rare victory over the Philistines. It was therefore another place of hallowed associations, but it, too, had been debased into the site of a pagan sanctuary.

Tabor means 'a lofty place'. This is doubtless a play on words, since this flat-topped mountain would most probably be the site of a pagan high place. Figuratively, the names referred to the high and lofty position of the priests and rulers, who had used their prominence to make themselves a snare to the people. The use of snares and nets was typical, since these mountains would be much frequented by hunters.

V2: The Hebrew of the first part of the verse is difficult, as is seen in the differing translations offered by various versions.

a) **The revolters are deeply involved in slaughter** (NIV: 'the rebels are deep in slaughter'). Some, including Calvin, say this refers to the elaborate sacrificial worship: their hearts were completely hardened so that their depravity was incurable. Others connect it with the murder and bloodshed which was part of the heathen regime, perhaps particularly that associated with the establishment of the house of Jehu, which was done in the name of religion (*1 Kings* 10:16). Leon Wood thinks it refers to the slaughter of a people handed over to ruin by God.

Though I rebuke them all. The speaker here may be God, who, through the prophets, continually rebukes their behaviour. Attention is drawn to their rejection of the prophetic messengers. Among these Elijah and Elisha, with their ministries accompanied by signs and miracles, were most notable.

b) The RSV follows a different reading of the Hebrew consonants, to render the verse '**they have made deep the pit of Shittim, but I will chastise all of them.** Shittim, or Acacia, was the name of the camp in Baal Peor where in the time of Moses the children of Israel had committed immorality with the women of Moab. The meaning may be that the snare is as subtle and destructive as that suggested to the Moabites by the false prophet Balaam, which led to sin and severe punishment (*Num.* 25, 31:16). It could also mean that the pit of sin first dug by the adultery (both physical and spiritual) at Baal Peor had since been dug deeper by successive generations. The last part of the verse is then a reminder that the Lord would punish them as severely as at Baal Peor. In fact, Israel would cease to be a kingdom at all. Only a remnant would be left.

V3: **Not hidden.** The prosperity of the reign of Jeroboam II had given rise to the false notion that God, as if unaware Israel's sin, would not judge it. Such an idea is firmly repudiated here. The nation had turned to prostitution, as at Baal Peor, and is seen as corrupt before God.

V4: Their deeds demonstrated that they were intent in their rebellion against God. People show by their deeds the intents of their hearts (*Mark* 7:20–23, *Luke* 6:43–45). These people were set upon their sin, enslaved to a spirit of prostitution and, like Gomer, had no intention of repenting (see 4:12).

V5: **The pride of Israel** may refer to God himself, who should have been the nation's pride and joy. As in 4:1, he would testify against them. But pride might refer to the arrogance of the nation (as in NIV). Calvin comments that the prophet no doubt applies the word 'pride' to their contempt of instruction: they were so swollen with vain confidence that they thought the prophets wronged them in rebuking them. The Lutheran commentator Theodore Laetsch sees a reference to the objects of the nation's pride that had taken the place of God. It is possible that a word play here includes both ideas.

Israel and Ephraim stumble. The pride of Ephraim had been demonstrated in the time of Gideon (*Judg.* 8:1) and Jephthah (*Judg.* 12:1). The tribe's importance had been promised in Jacob's blessing of Joseph's sons (*Gen.* 48:19); and Jeroboam I, from Ephraim, had become the first king of the independent Northern Kingdom of Israel.

Judah also stumbles. This part of the prophecy was not to be fulfilled immediately. Though faced with the terrible and inescapable example of Israel, Judah did not heed the warning of the prophets and repent. Even the considerable reformation under King Hezekiah and temporary deliverance from the Assyrian threat did not reach the hearts of the people and seems to have been later spoiled by the king's pride. Josiah's reformation was undoubtedly more thorough, and the king personally was very sincere. But the prophet Jeremiah indicates that the popular reaction to it was one of external correctness, not of heart repentance (*Jer.* 3:10).

V6: This further demonstrates that zeal shown in external forms of religion may be vain. Their lavish sacrifices were not in themselves well pleasing to God, as the Lord had shown at an earlier time to Saul (*1 Sam.* 15:22). The same delusion existed in Judah (*Mic.* 6:6–8), although that nation was not at this time as apostate as Israel.

Men may indeed seek the Lord and not find him, when they do not seek him in accordance with the revelation he has given. Deuteronomy 4:29 makes clear that men are to seek the Lord with all their heart, and Israel was not doing this (see 10:2). Psalm 66:18, too, warns that God does not hear prayer when there is iniquity in the heart. As we face this challenge, we must surely be convinced that salvation is wholly by the grace of God; for who, except the Lord Jesus, is so single-minded?

V7: **Treacherously** (NIV: 'unfaithful'). The nation was dealing as faithlessly with God as Gomer had dealt with Hosea. They had given birth to illegitimate children by taking wives from among their heathen neighbours. But this also illustrated their spiritual condition: they were behaving as those who did not know the desires or requirements of the Lord. The children were illegitimate, since they had made their parents' sins their own.

The new moon may refer to the new moon festival, which had assumed great prominence and would herald their forthcoming destruction; or it may refer to a short space of time.

Heritage (NIV: 'fields') may mean either their tribal territories, which would soon be overrun by invaders; or their individual fields presently overflowing with abundance, which would soon be devoured.

V8: **The ram's horn** (*shophar*) was the curved animal-horn trumpet. The **trumpet** was usually of brass or metal. Both were instruments used to warn of approaching danger.

Gibeah was a frontier town of Judah; **Ramah**, a frontier town of the Northern Kingdom. Both, in the tribal territory of Benjamin, were elevated places suitable for the sounding of warning. Some expositors suggest that naming these two towns emphasised the warning to both kingdoms.

Beth Aven may refer to Bethel (as in 4:15).

Look **behind you, O Benjamin** (NIV: 'lead on, Benjamin'). The different readings point to the difficulty of the text. In favour of the latter, it is suggested (cf. *Judg.* 5:14) that this was the tribe's war cry. The general sense is clear enough: it warns of the military dangers soon to come. Benjamin is addressed as being the part of Judah in closest proximity to Israel.

V9: Calvin interprets: 'I will not correct Israel as heretofore, for they have in various ways been chastised and not repented. I will now therefore lay aside these paternal corrections, for I have in vain applied such remedies: I will henceforth correct Israel that they shall be entirely destroyed.' This activity of God would no longer be the discipline of a father, but the sentence of the judge. This national judgement does not mean that every individual would be lost. Hosea's prophecy, though pronouncing fearsome judgement, does not entirely close the door to hope.

Among the tribes. The sentence was sure and had been declared to the whole nation. There was no appeal from this decree.

FOR MEDITATION

1. Outline for the whole chapter:
   a) The *witness to Ephraim* (vv1–7).
   b) The *warning of wrath* (vv8–14).
   c) The *withdrawal of grace* (v15).

2. Since Hosea so frequently emphasises the danger of religious institutions which have gone wrong, we should be careful to

avoid this snare. We need to watch personally, lest public and private devotions become an institution rather than a communion. The warning against losing first love given to the church at Ephesus (*Rev.* 2:1–5) must continually be borne in mind by those who consider themselves sound in doctrine, faith, and observance of Christian duties. We ought to observe the warning of Henry Scougal that:

> the severities of a holy life and that constant watch we are compelled to keep over our own hearts and ways, are very troublesome to those who are ruled and acted upon only by an external law, and have no law in their minds inclining them to the performance of their duty: but where divine love possesses the soul, it stands as a sentinel to keep out everything which may offend the Beloved, and doth disdainfully dismiss those temptations which assault it: it complieth cheerfully, not only with explicit commands, but with the most secret notices of the Beloved's pleasure, and is ingenious in discovering what will be most grateful and acceptable to him: it makes mortification and self-denial change their harsh and dreadful names, and become easy, sweet, and delightful things.[1]

It is clear from this that only a continual lively sense of the love of God can ensure a religion acceptable to God and man alike. No wonder Paul prays that the church may above everything else grow to know more of Christ's love (*Eph.* 3:14–21). Pray that the Lord will enlarge the heart (*Psa.* 119:32).

3. V2: The human heart by nature gets set upon the wrong things; we need to guard our hearts with all diligence (*Prov.* 4:23). The Scriptures remind us that though Christians have a new heart, we must put off the old man with its deeds (*Eph.* 4:22), lay aside all wickedness (*James* 1:21), and not allow sin

---

[1] In *The Life of God in the Soul of Man* (Tain, Ross-shire, U.K.: Christian Focus Publications, 1996 ed.) p.78.

to have dominion over us (*Rom.* 6:14). This is the continuing work of the Holy Spirit in the life of the believer.

4. V2: *Involved in slaughter.* In the modern world, life has become cheap. Reckless drivers, careless industrialists, and produceres of sub-standard goods endanger life. Some see abortion as an easy way out of parental responsibilities; many parents are too busy or too idle and thoughtless to concern themselves with their children's spiritual, moral, and physical welfare. But as Christians, we have responsibilities to those around us. It is easy to 'pass by on the other side', like the priest and the Levite in Jesus' parable of the good Samaritan. Are we salt and light in our society (*Matt.* 5:13–16)?

5. The prophet had to rebuke! Whilst we are not to become continual complainers or heartless judges, as Christians, we have a responsibility to raise our voice against evil when we see it. As individuals, we should be ready to:

a) make a stand for Christian values in society, as Elijah stood up to Ahab in the matter of Naboth's vineyard, and as John the Baptist stood up to Herod for his adulterous relationship with Herodias, though this ultimately cost him his head.

b) make a stand for purity of life and doctrine in the church (*Gal.* 6:1, *1 Tim.* 1:3–4, 18–20, *Jude* 3).

c) work to improve the conditions in which others live. One example of this is the work against the unscrupulous use of child labour in some Third World countries. But it is not enough to denounce. We should be ready to help where possible in practical ways with resources.

We must ask ourselves: Have I stood up for the truth lately? I may be spineless – or all spikes. Neither attitude is Christlike.

6. The RSV reading of *the pit at Acacia* reminds us of the destructiveness of lust, and we have another sad warning in the

story of Samson. We need to be on the watch against the false prophets of the day who hatch schemes like that of Balaam to turn God's people aside from his way by encouraging lust. Today self-control and self-discipline are continually talked down, and the cult of self-fulfilment dominates. Our young people particularly are subject to this pressure. How ardent should we be in praying for them and offering them a better way!

7. V3: The ways of God's people are not hidden from him (*Heb.* 4:13), even if I appear to be prospering in my sin. The thought that we can hide is monstrous self-deception. But how comforting is the thought that his eye is always upon me if I seek to walk with him (*Psa.* 32:8). Read Psalm 139. Consider also 2 Chronicles 16:9, Psalm 33:18; 34:15, and 1 Peter 3:11–12.

8. *The pride of Israel.* Pride brings down upon us dangers against which God has warned. Notice some of the dangers of pride:

a) complacency, as when Samson did not realise that the Spirit of God had departed from him (*Judg.* 16:20);

b) compromise, as when Hezekiah was flattered by the attentions of the Babylonian ambassadors (*Isa.* 39);

c) prayerlessness, as when Asa did not turn to the Lord in his afflictions because of the pride of his heart (*2 Chron.* 16:10, 12);

d) apostasy, as when Saul turned to the medium of Endor rather than cast himself upon God (*1 Sam.* 28);

e) independence, which brought the prodigal son near to destruction.

Do not be haughty, but fear (*Rom.* 11:20.). One of our greatest dangers is spiritual pride, which will do anything rather than submit to the Lord and reach out the beggar's hand for grace.

9. The Lord's knowledge of Israel's failing should remind us that he knows our failings too, yet he will never break his

covenant with us. The promise of 2 Chronicles 7:14 holds for us. If the people who are called by his name will humble themselves and pray, and seek his face, and turn from their wicked ways, then he will hear! His faithfulness must always be the ground of our assurance (*1 Cor.* 1:8–9).

10. V6: This verse contains a warning against superficial experiences of God for which there is no warrant in Scripture. In the case of any such experience we should ask, Where did this come from? God says he will be found where there is conviction of sin, humility of heart, repentance and faith in the Lord Jesus Christ. He is not there merely to make us feel good!

11. V7: A man alienated from God will beget strange children. Spiritually we shall bring forth after our kind (*Gen.* 1:24). My religious faith is not for me alone. It will affect my children, both in their character now and in their eternal destiny. Children cannot be saved by their parents' faith, but the Lord in his mercy may use that faith to bring the children to faith in him.

12. A *new moon shall destroy them.* We do not know how much time we have. Now is the day of salvation (*2 Cor.* 6:2)!

13. John Calvin's prayer on these verses:

> Grant, Almighty God, that as we are already by nature the children of wrath, and yet thou hast deigned to receive us into favour and hast set before us a sacred pledge of thy favour in thine only-begotten Son, and that as we have not yet ceased often to provoke thy wrath against us and also to fall away by shameful perfidy from the covenant thou hast made with us, – O grant that being at least touched by thy admonitions, we may not harden our hearts in wickedness, but be pliant and teachable and thus endeavour to return into favour with thee,

that through the interceding sacrifice of thy Son we may find thee a propitious Father, and be for the future so wholly devoted to thee that those who shall follow and survive us may be confirmed in the worship of thy majesty, and in true religion, through the same Jesus Christ Our Lord. Amen.

Chapter 5:10–15

'They will not listen!'

The last part of the chapter focuses more on the failure of Judah, as though to warn her against the conceit that she was better than the Northern Kingdom. Both kingdoms are warned of the impending judgement.

V10: Some suggest that the reference to removing a landmark may have in view the willingness of Judah to take advantage of the Northern Kingdom by seizing territory; but it more probably refers to the nobles' oppression of the lesser landowners, which reduced many to slavery. Micah shows special interest in this aspect of Judah's sin (*Mic.*2:2). Those who removed landmarks were regarded as the lowest kind of thieves (*Deut.* 19:14; 27:27).

The phrase 'removing landmarks' apparently could also refer metaphorically to the setting aside of the ancient and well-tried standards, and applied particularly to the spiritual landmarks given by God. Perhaps here it referred to the blatant way Ahaz turned from God's law. He 'encouraged moral decline' and 'had been continually unfaithful to the LORD' (*2 Chron.* 28:19).

I will pour out my wrath. Previously the prophet had spoken of Judah in a better light and warned her of becoming involved in sinful ways. Here it is made very clear that unless the people heeded the warning, they too would be judged. Their religious institutions had not broken down completely, but that did not mean they could sit securely and preen themselves; the spiritual need of Judah, too, was great.

We cannot date this prophecy precisely, but we can work out the background. In Judah during the long reigns of Uzziah and his son Jotham, religion had been relatively orthodox. Under Ahaz the nation had declined seriously, but this was followed by a revival largely inspired by King Hezekiah and the prophet Isaiah. The rapid decline in the reign of Manasseh, however, indicates that this revival had been largely superficial for the majority of the people. God and the prophets saw through the façade to their wayward affections, demonstrated in their easy acceptance of pagan innovations. The rulers, who oppressed the poor, were particularly culpable.

Like water may be a reminder of the judgement of the Flood. It challenges the people concerning the awfulness of their sin in the sight of God. Isaiah likens the Assyrian invasion to a flood (ch. 8).

V11: Hosea saw the Northern Kingdom as broken by the judgement of God. The last part of the verse has presented difficulty for translators, as is seen by the different translations offered.

He willingly walked by *human* precept (NKJ) understands a rare Hebrew word (found elsewhere only in Isaiah 28:10) as 'precepts', which is its obvious meaning in Isaiah. **Intent on pursuing idols** (NIV) follows the Septuagint, which translates the word as 'vanities'.

The outcome reveals little difference, since the precepts in view are generally taken to be those of Jeroboam I: the establishment of the worship of the golden calves at Bethel and Dan at the institution of the Northern Kingdom.

Another possible reading suggests that Ephraim is an oppressor, trampling on justice and doggedly pursuing what is worthless.

V12: The judicial work of God will be like moth and rottenness. Both analogies indicate a process which is gradual but deadly.

V13: **Sickness** carries with it the thought of consuming weakness. **Wound** implies that it is both deep and festering. Both words indicate a desperate condition. When at last Ephraim was compelled to admit her plight, she turned not to the Lord, but to the Assyrian king.

King Jareb. The Hebrew may be read as 'the king who contends' or possibly, with a slight amendment, 'the great king', which was a common way of addressing an overlord of lesser kings. Some have suggested that the subject of the phrase should be Judah, and it is clear that Ahaz did seek Assyrian aid when faced by the alliance of Syria and Israel (*Isa.* 7–9, *2 Kings* 16: 6–9, *2 Chron.* 28:16). The duplicity of Assyria in pretending to support both Israel and Judah, and the foolishness of both kingdoms in seeking an alliance with Assyria are well illustrated here.

After the death of Jeroboam II, the Northern Kingdom had gone into rapid decline and the threat from Assyria began to increase. Israel's Menahem became a tributary king. After his death, Pekah joined forces with the Syrian king, Rezin, in an attempt to form a Palestinian coalition against Assyria. Judah refused to join this triple alliance, and Ahaz, Judah's king, in face of the threat of force by Rezin and Pekah, called for Assyrian aid. It was not long before the Northern Kingdom crumbled under the Assyrian attack.

The prophet is telling both Israel and Judah that Assyria was no answer to their problems and would not be able to **cure** or **heal**. Isaiah 1 uses the same symbolism of sickness and healing: that the real problem was their sin, and the Lord alone could heal. This reflects the truth taught long before, that 'I *am* the LORD who heals you' (*Exod.* 15:26).

V14: The Lord is seen here as a lion who would consume both Ephraim and Judah, and none would be able to snatch away his prey. Isaiah 10:5 makes clear that his instrument would be

Assyria. In feverishly seeking aid from that source, they were looking to a false saviour.

V15: This speaks of a divine withdrawal until they were prepared to acknowledge their sin and seek the Lord's help.

In their affliction they will earnestly seek Me. Even in the midst of the awesome threats of judgement there is a word of hope. Some versions connect this with the first three verses of chapter 6, as though these were the voice of their seeking. There is no evidence for this, though there may be a close connection, whether the appeal is read as the orthodox but superficial response of the people, or as the tender appeal of the prophet.

FOR MEDITATION

1. Outline for these verses:
   a) A day of *reckoning* pronounced.
   b) A day of *restoration* promised.
   c) A day of *repentance* pursued.

The love of God does not compromise his holiness, but his great work is to establish both. This truth is most perfectly demonstrated at the cross (*Rom.* 3:26).

2. *Landmarks.* The Lord attached great importance to the 'landmarks' of his law. The perfect obedience of the life of Jesus and the atoning significance of his death are the ultimate divine witness to this. We discard his standards at our own peril. They are a work of grace intended to keep us on the right path. Among those landmarks is a great concern for social justice, which is enshrined in the second of the great commandments: 'You shall love your neighbour as yourself.'

3. The judgements of God are progressively severe. A process of gradual weakening is followed by the lion of sudden calamity.

The worst judgement of all is when God withdraws himself and gives men up to their sinful ways (*Rom.* 1:26). We should be wise to repent as soon as we see the moth, realising that it is only the forbearance of God that restrains the final judgement. The progressive work of judgement is a call to repent (see *Amos* 4:6–12).

4. V13: We are warned against looking for help in the wrong places. We can deplore the folly of the gambler who believes that one more bet will solve all his problems, yet we are prone to trust in our own efforts or in other fallible men. Repentance towards God is the only solution. The tortuous efforts of Israel and Judah to save themselves testify to the folly and failure of mankind. The real problem is in the heart of man and can be solved only by the grace of God.

5. One way in which God makes men see their folly is the withdrawal of his gracious help. By this method of discipline, the true believer will be brought to his senses. King Alfred the Great had this experience, which he described as follows:

> *When in such strife my mind will forget*
> *Its light and its life in worldly regret,*
> *And through the night of this world doth grope*
> *Lost to the light of heavenly hope.*
> *Thus it has now befallen my mind,*
> *I know no more how God's goodness to find,*
> *But I moan in my grief, troubled and tossed,*
> *Needing relief for the world I have lost.*[1]

Then, when men see their guilt and seek his face, they find that he is at hand to deliver (*Jer.* 29:13). 'You will seek Me and find *Me*, when you search for Me with all your heart.'

[1] In *The Whole Works of Alfred the Great, Vol. 1* (New York: AMS Press, 1969), p.174.

A prayer of Alfred shows appreciation of this truth:

I implore thee, Lord, to receive me, thy fugitive, since I was once formerly thine and deserted from thee to the devil, and fulfilled his will, enduring much misery in his service. But if it seems to thee that I have long enough endured the pains . . . please receive me, thine own servant. Never again let me go, now that I have sought thee.[2]

6. John Calvin: 'The prophet shows here that exile, though very bitter to Israel would yet be useful, as when the physician gives a bitter draught to cure an inveterate disease. So, the prophet shows that the punishment would be useful, even pleasant, however bitter it might be for a time.'

This is the teaching of Hebrews 12:5–13. Paul reminds us that all things work together for the good of those who love God (*Rom.* 8:28), and he also speaks of the good and perfect and acceptable will of God (*Rom.* 12:2). There will be disciplines along our Christian path, and some of these will be very painful. But by these the power of indwelling sin within us will be weakened and our hearts disposed to seek earnestly the Lord, who is the source of all our good. In the midst of them we must learn to cast ourselves upon God, as Alfred did. We need to seek the help of the Holy Spirit to accomplish this.

---

[2] In *The Whole Works of Alfred the Great, Vol.2* (New York: AMS Press, 1969), pp.88–89.

Chapter 6:1–3

An Exhortation to Repentance

V1: Some expositors connect this with 5:15, as do the RSV and also Leon Wood in his commentary: 'In their affliction they will seek me early saying "Come let us return to the Lord".' This follows the approach of the Septuagint, but there is no support for it in the Hebrew.

Apart from this linking with the previous chapter, the appeal may be read in two ways:

a) It reads best as the prophet's response to the tender purpose of God expressed in 5:15. He pleads with the people to return to God by exalting the divine mercy, bringing assurance that God will restore. Any grounds for mercy and acceptance must be found in the compassion of the offended God, and not in some fancied merit of the repentant one. The covenant name of God is used here to make clear that the ground of the appeal is the undeserved covenant mercy of God.

He has torn. The same word is found in 5:14. It is acknowledged that the trouble has come from the hand of God as his discipline. Anyone in whom the Spirit of God is at work comes to learn that his misfortunes are in fact the kindliness of heavenly discipline correcting his sins in order to develop his relationship with God. Before there can be restoration, we must recognise that we deserve God's displeasure.

He will heal, because he is the God who delights in mercy. The power, sovereignty and mercy of God are all in view here. He has the right and the ability both to wound and to heal.

Nebuchadnezzar recognised this absolute divine sovereignty when he cried, 'He does according to His will in the army of heaven and *among* the inhabitants of earth. No one can restrain His hand or say to Him, "What have you done?"' (*Dan.* 4:35).

He will bind us up. The healing indicates his power, the binding up, his tenderness and skill. God's dealings with us perfectly express the compassion of a true father with a stubborn and disobedient child: firm discipline and great compassion.

V2: **After two days; on the third day.** The expression usually indicates a short passage of time; here it illustrates the mercy of God and his readiness to forgive. In this verse it may have Messianic undertones, anticipating the resurrection of the Lord Jesus Christ. Calvin remarks: 'Though exile seems to be like the sepulchre where putridity awaits us, yet the Lord will, by his ineffable power, overcome whatever seems to obstruct our restoration.'

He will raise us up. The nation brought so low, as his earlier threatening foretold, could be raised only by a display of Almighty grace and power.

We may live in His sight. The eye of God is upon us for good (*Psa.* 2:8).

V3 **Let us know. Let us pursue the knowledge of the LORD** (NIV: 'Let us acknowledge the Lord'). The repentant ones respond enthusiastically. When one is brought into a real relationship with God, one longs to grow in it and is inspired to make one's calling and election sure (*2 Pet.* 1:4–10)

His going forth. The Lord's intervention on behalf of his people is as sure as day follows night. The night of calamity will be transcended by the sunshine of the divine grace, as Calvin remarks: 'Though there is now, on every side, horrible darkness, yet the Lord will manifest his goodness to us, even though it may not immediately appear.'

Rain; latter and former rain. The two rainy seasons, the winter rain and spring showers, accounted for the region's great fertility, and the failure of these rains was a major disaster. Rain is a common symbol for the Holy Spirit in the Old Testament (*Isa.* 43:19–20; 44:3, *Ezek.* 34:26).

b) Some expositors regard these verses as an expression of Israel's superficiality, which is condemned by God in 6:4. According to this view, they express the casual way in which Israel expected restoration, without any awareness of the greatness of their sin, as though forgiveness were a right. Paul speaks of this frame of mind which would want to claim mercy without due consideration of the moral demands of repentance (*Rom.* 2:4–5). The verses, when read in this way, serve as a solemn reminder that presumptuous hearts may use the language of repentance without the essential spiritual understanding of what is involved, which is the gift of the Holy Spirit.

FOR MEDITATION

1. Outline of the section:
   a) The *summons of the caring prophet.*
   b) The *smiting of an offended God.*
   c) The *succour of redeeming grace.*

2. The *divine invitations.* The redeeming grace of God is freely offered to the repentant sinner. This offer has many aspects:
   a) An invitation to reason (*Isa.* 1:18). God calls us to recognise the awfulness of sin and to realise that he alone can cleanse. In the Old Testament, the sacrificial system was ordained to reflect this.
   b) An invitation to rest (*Matt.* 11:28). God, in Christ, promises to relieve the burdened conscience and to give peace in the face of the responsibilities of life and the overwhelming

power of temptation. He invites us to take the yoke of his authority which will be made light by the grace of his unfailing presence.

c) *An invitation to refreshment* (*John* 7:37). In Scripture the life of the believer is pictured in terms of the Exodus: the pilgrim is called out of bondage to the heavenly city, for here we have no continuing city. To the heavenly citizen, this earthly life is likened to the passage through the wilderness, and the resources, like those of Israel of old, must be supernatural. God's people are dependent upon the manna from heaven and the water from the smitten rock (*John* 6:36, *1 Cor.* 10:4).

d) *An invitation to return* (*Hos.* 6:1). We can return to God with confidence because he invites us. His love and power are sufficient to heal, but we must realise that he has smitten, sent the circumstances of distress, so that we might be stopped in our tracks, see our need, and turn to him.

All these benefits come to believers in both Old and New Testaments on the grounds of the finished work of Christ, who died as their substitute on the cross (*Rom.* 3:24 –26).

3. Vv 1–2: The activity of God applies beautifully to the wonder of our salvation, but it also recalls God's chastening of our disobedience. He is the one who has 'torn' and 'smites', but he is the one who restores. He:

Heals. He is the great physician (*Mark* 2:17).

Binds up. He is infinite in gentleness and tender love (*Luke* 4:18, *Isa.* 61:1).

Revives. He is the resurrection and the life (*John* 11:25–26) and brings life out of death (*Eph.* 2:1).

Raises up. Those who have fallen under the bondage of sin and are being sucked down into the 'miry pit' are raised up to sit in heavenly places in Christ Jesus (*Psa.* 40:2–3, *Eph.* 2:7, *Col.* 3:1).

4. V2: The wonder of the delight of living in his sight is expressed in Psalm 139, which speaks of God's love (*Exod.* 3:7–8); his guidance (*Psa.* 32:8); our security (*Matt.* 10:29–31); and our obedience (*Psa.* 143:8). The sinner attempts to hide (*Gen.* 3:8), but the believer walks before the Lord (*Gen.* 17:1).

5. V3: The coming of God to our souls may be likened to the shining of the morning sun after the long dark night of sin (*Mal.* 4:2, *2 Cor.* 4:4–6, *1 Pet.* 2:9). This light is sure for the believer, as day follows night; therefore we should wait confidently for it in dark days (*Isa.* 50:10). It is a light which will grow day by day as we walk with the Lord (*Prov.* 4:18).

6. *He shall come as the former and the latter rain.* The Lord is the source of all the fruitfulness of believers. His grace produces transformation (*Isa.* 35) and the stability and vitality of the godly man (*Jer.* 17:8). Jesus speaks of this in John 4:14 and 7:37–39. We must ask whether this is our experience and pray that God in his grace will make it so.

7. If these verses are to be understood as an example of presumption on the mercy of God, we must pay careful heed to their warning and ask ourselves: Do I abuse the mercy of God by continuing in my sin, casually promising that I will do something about it 'one day'? Do I assume that God, being a God of mercy, will never judge?

If we truly love the Lord and take his Word seriously, we shall not fall into these errors. Repentance will never be a shallow matter.

John 14:15–21 stresses the positive side of walking with God.

Chapter 6:4–11a

'What Shall I Do?' Is God Ever Puzzled?

These verses are mainly concerned with the fickleness and blood-guiltiness of Israel.

V4: **Ephraim** stands here for the whole Northern Kingdom; **Judah** is the Southern Kingdom.

Calvin comments: 'Now God by these words intimates that he had tried all remedies and found them useless: you are wholly incurable, inexcusable and altogether past hope.' Isaiah expresses the same opinion about Judah (*Isa.* 1:5; 5:4).

Here Hosea is speaking of both kingdoms, although the history of Judah was to run on for much longer than that of Israel. Judah enjoyed two periods of extensive reform under Hezekiah (729–686 B.C.) and Josiah (639–609 B.C.), but the Lord knew the evil hearts of the majority of the people even in the south. At the time of Josiah's reforms, Jeremiah spoke of the feigned repentance of the people (*Jer.* 3:10). The externals of public worship were put right, and even morality was to some extent reformed, but there was no change in the heart of the people. Jeremiah uses the analogy of the unfaithful wife (*Jer.* 3:20).

What shall I do? This does not mean that God is surprised or puzzled by human behaviour. But here a human form of speech expresses his grief at the hardness of heart which persists in spite of all the correction he has given to prevent them from rushing headlong into ruin. The disasters which were to come upon them were in no way due to any failure of love or lack of endeavour on the Lord's part. He had left nothing undone which could have been done. The whole prophecy shows that God knew exactly what he would do (to find the answer we must turn to chapter 14).

Faithfulness (NIV: 'love') translates the Hebrew *hesed*, which frequently refers to the covenant love of God but can also refer to the response of God's people to his electing grace. It is then to be demonstrated in true worship, in accordance with what God has revealed, and the merciful attitudes to others which he has shown towards them (see again 2:20).

Morning cloud and **early dew** both represent something that does not last long. Like these, the repentance and religious professions of the people soon faded and disappeared.

V5: Hewn *them* by the prophets; slain them by the words of my mouth. The people had been denounced by the prophets, the Lord's spokesmen, in the strongest possible language, and powerfully warned of the disaster into which they were heading.

Your judgements (NIV is more clear: 'my judgements'): God's judgements of them are compared to lightning flashing (NIV) as their sin was exposed and their judgement declared. They could not have any doubt as to what their end would be. They were set on their course of destruction with eyes wide open.

V6: In this one verse, later quoted by the Lord Jesus Christ (*Matt.* 9:13; 12:7), Hosea effectively summarises the essential prophetic message. God was not to be appeased by elaborate sacrificial rituals, but would only accept the worship of sincere hearts expressing themselves in obedience to the divine law and love for fellow men (cf. *1 Sam.* 15:22, *Amos* 5:21–24, *Mic.* 6:6–8, *Isa.* 1:11–20, *Jer.* 7:21–24).

As Isaiah expressed it (*Isa.* 29:13) the Jews were a people who were worshipping God with their lips but their hearts were far from him. On occasion, they gloried in the uniqueness of the prophetic message, but they did not heed it and continued in their covetous ways (*Ezek.* 33:30–32, *Isa.* 66:3). The Lord Jesus had spoken of such hypocrisy (*Matt.* 23:29–30); Paul denounced the Jews of his day in the same strain (*Rom.* 10:2–3).

Some critics have seen here evidence of a conflict between the prophets and the whole idea of sacrifice, but this conclusion stems from a wilful literalism. The prophets are denouncing the sins of immorality, idolatry, and self-righteousness, which violate the covenant and invalidate the sacrifices. As George Adam Smith comments in *The Book of the Twelve Prophets*: 'What could make repentance so easy as the belief that forgiveness could be won simply by offering sacrifices?'

V7: Many approaches have been made to the translation and exposition here: **like men** (NKJ, AV); **as at Adam** (RSV, and preferred by Michael Eaton); **like Adam** (NIV; also NKJ and AV margins, followed by Matthew Henry and J.B. Phillips). 'They have walked over the covenant as if it were dirt' has also been suggested as possible.

If the reading 'like Adam' is adopted, the emphasis is on identification with Adam in the personal folly and unreasonable rebellion of a privileged person. The objections raised against this interpretation are that no covenant with Adam is mentioned in Genesis, and Hosea would not be familiar with the story of Adam. But there are no objective grounds for the view that the prophet did not know the story of Adam, since he shows familiarity with other patriarchal stories. Furthermore, the covenant idea was so familiar by the time of Hosea that it would not be surprising if he conceived of Adam's sin as a breach of covenant.

Adam was also a city about eighteen miles from Jericho, near where the waters of the Jordan were held back. It was in the territory of Gilead, so the reference may be related to what follows in verses 8–9, drawing attention to some recent incident of an atrocious killing at the instigation of the priests. 2 Kings 15:25 clearly indicates that Gileadites were involved in the murder of Pekahiah, which might be referred to in verse 8.

It is possible that the prophet deliberately intended a double meaning, since the word 'transgress' can also be used of crossing a river. Hosea may have chosen the name Adam to call to mind that at the very time of the covenant renewal (*Josh.* 3:16; 5:1–12) the sin of Achan revealed the unchanging heart of Israel (*Josh.* 6:18–19; 7:1–11). He had already referred to the valley of Achor (2:15), so this incident could well have been in his mind. At the same time, the name Adam referred back to the father of the human race as the father of all covenant breaking.

The sense is clear enough: their sin was deep rooted and deliberate. They were guilty of continual treachery.

There may refer to an incident at Adam; or to Gilead, mentioned in verse 8, possibly Ramoth Gilead, which was a Levitical city; or to any sanctuary where their rituals were conducted. Some have argued that it means 'in the matter of offering sacrifices, rather than true worship'. Matthew Henry, who adopts the reading 'like Adam', applies it to the Garden of Eden, where Adam first sinned.

V8: Gilead was an area east of Jordan where Jephthah, the judge, had lived. The town of Ramoth Gilead may be intended, since that was a Levitical city and a city of refuge, but now infamous for murder and evil.

V9: On the way (NIV: 'road') **to Shechem.** The Hebrew could literally mean 'with the shoulder'. Calvin insisted that it should be read 'by consent' as men stood shoulder to shoulder in conspiracy. However, the place name has much to commend it as we view its associations:

It was the first place in the promised land where Jacob had attempted settlement, and had a history of violence which could be regarded as typical of Israel's failure (*Gen.* 34, *Judg.* 9).

It was the place of the renewal of the covenant promise to Abraham (*Gen.* 12:7).

Shechem was where Jacob raised an altar to the God of Israel (*Gen.* 33:20); he brought the tribe together to renew the covenant (*Josh.* 8:30–35): he appointed it to be a city of refuge (*Josh.* 20:7); and he again brought the people together to this place to renew the covenant before his death (*Josh.* 24).

It was where the northern tribes formally rejected Rehoboam, the son of Solomon, as king and made Jeroboam their ruler (*1 Kings* 12:1–19).

For a time it became the capital of the Northern Kingdom (*1 Kings* 12:35). But this place of hallowed associations became a place of apostasy, violence and immorality.

V10: The prophet, speaking in the name of God, saw not only the afflictions of the people but also their great wickedness, which he again called 'prostitution'. The people were defiled, and their sacrificial system, rightly understood, taught them that cleansing could come only by the gracious provision of God, when they were sufficiently humbled to turn to him.

V11: The main denunciation has been against Israel, but Judah is warned again. The harvest of sin must inevitably be reaped. Judah had already been warned by Hosea (4:15, 17; 5:5, 13–14).

The last part of this verse is usually associated with the following chapter.

FOR MEDITATION

1. Outline for chapter 6:1–6:
   a) An *earnest appeal.* There is an offer of grace (cf. *Isa.* 1:18, *Matt.* 11:28–30).

b) An *enlightened analysis.* The character of God is revealed
in justice and in grace. There must be recognition of his
wrath, and repentance to receive his grace.

c) An *encouraging assurance.* He will heal (cf. *Psa.* 30:5). His
mercy is 'super-abundant'(*Rom.* 5:15–17).

d) An *exposed affection.* The superficial response of the
people is exposed.

e) An *enduring allegiance.* God requires a loyalty which
matches his grace and can come only by the work of his
Spirit in our hearts. We are intended to be 'like him',
bearing his image.

2. Outline for chapters 6:1–7:2:
   a) An *exhortation to repentance* (6:1–3).
   b) An *examination of the heart of the nation* (6:4).
   c) An *explanation of the divine dealings* (6:5–6).
   d) An *exposure of the nation's sin* (6:7–7:2).

3. V4: God's compassionate concern over human waywardness
should draw us back to him, especially when we understand
properly the consequences of human rebellion and the price
paid for our redemption (*2 Cor.* 5:21, *1 Pet.* 3:18). The continual
abuse of grace and forbearance will lead to the outpouring of
irresistible wrath. The repetition of this truth bears witness to
its importance. God repeats it time and again, as we might
repeat a lesson to a small child. The Apostle Paul could use the
same blend of compassionate appeal and threat (*2 Cor.* 10).

4. V4: We are reminded that the covenant love of God is no
uncertain quantity, as the Apostle Peter learned the hard way
(*Luke* 22:32). Praise God that the Lord Jesus prays for his people
that their faith will not fail. If he did not confirm us to the end,
we would undoubtedly fall by the wayside. But we can be sure
of his faithfulness (*1 Cor.* 1:8–9, *Phil.* 1:6, *1 Pet.* 5:10).

5. We must not expect the Bible to provide us with 'mushy' comfort. God is holy, and his holy love will not allow us to become spoilt children. The Word of God will sometimes 'hew us' (*Heb.* 4:12). Part of its profitability is that it corrects (*2 Tim.* 3:16). When we are wayward, we must expect it to be like a fire or a hammer that breaks the rock in pieces (*Jer.* 23:29). When Jeremiah would have turned away from his task of challenging a rebellious people, he found the Word of God like a fire in his bones (*Jer.* 20:9).

Jesus said that he 'did not come to bring peace but a sword' (*Matt.* 10:34), and we must recognise this as we handle the Word of God. The Word as it uncovers the iniquity of our hearts will bring wounds of love. The preacher must nerve himself to this work of bringing conviction with compassion as well as courage. The Word must sometimes be the surgeon's knife before it can be the healing balm. But it can never be the opium of the people. It lives and gives life, and the bringing forth of new life is a painful business (*John* 16:21, *Gal.* 4:19). There will be times when the preaching of the Word will be painful to the preacher and to the hearer alike, but we must not shrink from either responsibility.

6. V5: *Judgements as the light.* God leaves men in no doubt about the fact, the nature or the consequences of sin. Judgement is a universal truth (*Rom.* 1:18:21, 28, 32), and the people of God are especially accountable, since they have the oracles of God (*Rom.* 2:1–3; 17–21; 3:1–2).

7. V7: *'Like men'* or *'like Adam'.* From the Bible there is no doubt that we are involved in the sin of Adam. The race fell with him morally and legally. We have come under condemnation and have become partakers in his waywardness (*Rom.* 5:12, 17–19). Though Israel of old enjoyed the privilege of being the chosen people of God, in their fickleness they behaved

like the rest of men. This is also true of the visible church. To be anything other than 'like men', we need a new birth, the regenerating Spirit of God bringing us to a living faith in the Lord Jesus Christ. So Thomas Boston writes:

> The soul, which was made upright in all its faculties, is now wholly disordered. The heart that was made according to God's own heart is now the reverse of it, a forge of evil imaginations, a sink of inordinate affections, and a storehouse of all impiety . . . Surely that corruption which is ingrained into our hearts, interwoven with our very natures, has sunk into the marrow of our souls and will never be cured but by a miracle of grace.[1]

8. V9: The people who enjoy the greatest privileges often become guilty of the foulest treacheries and the most grievous failures. Thus it was Judas, one of the twelve, who betrayed the Lord. And it was Peter who denied him. Yet in the face of so solemn a warning we are reminded of how the Lord prayed for Peter (*Luke* 22:32). It is only through the grace and the intercessions of our glorious covenant Head that we can have confidence (see *Rom.* 8:32–34). The fact that Jesus prayed for Peter and not for Judas confronts us with a mystery which should prompt us to intercede that God would have mercy upon us.

In our flesh there dwells nothing good (*Rom.* 7:18)! Truly in Christ we are called to be kings and priests unto God, but we can fulfil this holy calling only as we walk in continual dependence upon him. Our calling gives us no grounds for presumption. Pray especially for leaders, particularly the good ones. The devil would have them 'to sift them as wheat', and it is our privilege to be involved in the spiritual battle on their behalf.

---

[1] In *Human Nature in Its Fourfold State* (Edinburgh: Banner of Truth, 1997), pp.61–62.

9. V11: *The harvest.* The New Testament solemnly reminds us of the connection between sowing and reaping in the spiritual realm.

In the parables of the sower and of the wheat and the tares, we are challenged as to what we are doing with the Word of God day by day. What will the harvest be?

We shall reap whatever we sow. We may see this to some degree here and now in the 'works of the flesh' or the 'fruit of the Spirit' (*Gal.* 5:19–23), but there is an eternal harvest yet to come (*Gal.* 6:6–9).

10. The title of this study is a question which to some sounds foolish, but which in fact expresses the thoughts of many and therefore requires an answer. If God is sovereign, all wise, and all powerful, he is obviously never puzzled. He knows exactly what he is doing and will accomplish all that he purposes to do.

Psalm 33, especially verse 11, states the position of the Christian very beautifully.

Nebuchadnezzar learned the truth from his experience of the grace of God (*Dan.* 4:34–35). The fact that we do not always see or understand what God is doing puzzles some, and in their conceits they think that God must be puzzled too! What presumption! Ecclesiastes 5:2 fits the argument, though in its context it is applied to vows: 'For God *is* in heaven, and you on earth, therefore let your words be few.'

There are times when we should bow in wonder and worship!

Oh, the depth of the riches both of the wisdom and knowledge of God. How unsearchable *are* His judgements and His ways past finding out! 'For who has known the mind of the LORD? Or who has become His counsellor? Or who has first given to Him and it shall be repaid to him?' For of Him and through Him and to Him *are* all things, to whom *be* glory for ever, Amen (*Rom.* 11:33–36).

'Oh, that I knew where I might find Him' (*Job* 23:3) may sometimes express our puzzlement, but 'He knows the way that I take; *when* he has tested me, I shall come forth as gold' (*Job* 23:10) should express our assurance. We may be puzzled, but he is not and cannot be. We must learn to rest in that. He knows what he is doing! His people should find security in that (*Psa.* 121:2–5).

Chapter 7:1–16

'The Pride of Israel Testifies to His Face!'

The prophet here concentrates on the persistent nature of the sin of Israel.

V1: Many commentators take this with the last part of 6:11. It presents their wilful perseverance in sin in the face of the gracious willingness of God to forgive. Two significant words are used: **iniquity**, which carries the thought of perverseness and shows that the seat of the problem is in their nature, and **wickedness**, a general word for evil doings. The chapter enumerates various particulars of Israel's sins which are picturesquely described as 'grey hairs' – evidence of decline of which one may not at once be aware.

Ephraim probably indicates the whole country, and Samaria, the capital city.

Fraud (Heb.: *sheqer*) indicates lying in word and deed. In no sphere could the people be trusted. This was true not least in the realm of religion, where they professed to worship God but broke God's law, practised idolatry, and generally disregarded their covenant responsibilities. Their costly rituals were all an enormous lie.

A thief. All manner of dishonesty was rampant: exorbitant usury, false weights and measures, and monopoly trading, as well as the more blatant forms of robbery. The prophet doubtless included also the idea of robbing God, just as an unfaithful wife robs her husband. The Lord was betrothed to a nation of thieves!

A band of robbers. Some commentators say this refers to foreign invaders. Others think it refers to the corruption of the nation and the open robbery and violence on the highways (see 6:9). Both suggestions can be seen as the expression of the judgement of God.

V2: **They do not consider.** Because they were spiritually blind and enslaved by sin and their hearts inflamed with evil passions, they behaved without thought.

I remember all their wickedness. Part of spiritual enlightenment is to understand the reality of God's judgement. A holy God cannot behave as though sin had not been committed. Sin has its inevitable wages (*Rom.* 6:23).

Their own deeds have surrounded them (NIV: 'engulfed') (cf. *Prov.* 5:22). They had dug a pit for their own feet (*Prov.* 26:27). They fondly imagined that the Lord did not see (*Psa.* 94:7), but all the time the severity of the judgement was building up. They were being reserved for judgement until the time of their iniquity was full (*Gen.* 15:16, *Jude* 6). We need to be reminded that this concept of judgement is a doctrine of the Old Testament only, but is also clearly taught in the New. The messages of judgement for sin and salvation by grace are a common thread. The Saviour himself uttered the most solemn words about the judgement (e.g., *Matt.* 24:50–51).

They are before My face. All their sinful rebellion is under the consideration of the all-seeing and all-knowing God (*Heb.* 4:12–13). The rebounding of sinful acts is not accidental, but a part of the omniscient sovereign purpose of God, a warning of a final judgement yet to come. Matthew Henry points out that they should have seen the bands of foreign invaders as the consequential punishment of their rebellion against God and an objective reminder of the fact that their sins were already before his face.

V3: The nation was ready to please its king by committing evil. Evil in high places is a running sore (*Prov.* 29:12). When the rulers are corrupt, the servants become wicked. When Herod saw that his evil ways pleased the Jews, he was disposed to commit further evil (*Acts* 12:3). Both people and princes are held responsible before God.

V4: **Adulterers.** This was doubtless true in both the spiritual and the physical sense, though the emphasis here may be on the latter, since the emphasis of the section is on the enflaming of passions by strong drink.

Like an oven. Their lusts are likened to a heated oven so well stoked that it needs no further attention. The people not only prone to lust but desired it greedily, so that their madness was like a raging flame.

V5: **The day of our king** may refer to the king's birthday or to some other important royal festival. Under the influence of drink, the king made bosom companions of arrogant, scornful, and ungodly men instead of suppressing them, as a godly monarch should. Such a picture brings to mind Belshazzar (*Dan.* 5) and Rehoboam (*1 Kings* 12). The psalmist warns against sitting in the seat of the scornful (*Psa.* 1:2). The Bible is also full of solemn warnings against the vice of heavy drinking (*Prov.* 20:1). Habakkuk 2:15 denounces causing the drunkenness of a neighbour as a great crime.

V6: **They prepare their heart.** They were not only sinners, but were diligent sinners, stoking up their lusts by indulging evil thoughts. The figure of the oven is used again here.

While they lie in wait. They fed their passions by evil thoughts even while they were waiting to express them. We are reminded of the natural perversity of the human heart (*Jer.* 17:9, *Mark* 7:20–23). This is the way men go but for the restraining grace of God.

The last part of the verse presents a problem of translation, as is shown in the different translations:

Their baker sleeps all night (NKJ) has given rise to the suggestion that while the baker is asleep, the oven becomes overheated and burns out of control. A change in the Hebrew pointing gives the reading 'their anger sleeps all night' which is followed by the Septuagint and the NIV: **their passion smoulders all night.** Calvin points out that their wickedness was not a sudden impulse but had grown hot like an oven, which had been stoked by degrees.

V7: The thought of verse 4 is repeated, but the suggestion that **they have devoured their judges** may reflect, or prophesy, the political situation at the end of the Northern Kingdom. Zechariah, son of Jeroboam II, Shallum, Pekahiah, and Pekah were all assassinated in court intrigues within a period of twenty years from 752 B.C. (*2 Kings* 15:10, 14, 25, 30).

Even the extremities of their distress and trouble did not turn them back to God.

V8: **Ephraim has mixed himself.** Behind this is the idea of prostitution, which runs so strongly through the book (5:13 reflects political prostitution). The nation had lost its distinctiveness as the chosen people of God (cf. *Psa.* 106:35–39). After the death of Jeroboam II , the kings continually sought foreign support to bolster their very uncertain hold on power.

A cake unturned. The figure is of a cake burned on one side and not cooked on the other, so that it was good for nothing. We have a vivid image of instability and unbalanced extremes. Elijah, in an earlier day, had complained that the nation was attempting to lean to both sides (*1 Kings* 18:21).

V9: **Aliens have devoured his strength** could refer to the bribes necessary to buy off the Assyrian threat (*2 Kings* 15,19–20), as well as to the progressive inroads of heathen practices. The decline was both political and religious.

He does not know *it* (cf. v2). Their spiritual blindness caused them to be oblivious. One is reminded of Samson, who was unaware that the Lord had departed from him (*Judg.* 16:20).

Gray hairs are evidence of decreasing power, evident to others, but not to themselves. Calvin comments that Israel 'had been visited with so many evils that he was worn out, as it were, by old age; and after all, he had derived no benefit'.

V10: **The pride of Israel** (as in 5:5). This could refer to God, but the NIV translates it 'arrogance'. Matthew Henry states that 'under humbling providences, their hearts were still unhumbled and their lusts unmortified'.

The LORD their God. The aggravated nature of their sin is emphasised. Their sin was against the One who had chosen them in grace, with whom they had entered into covenant, and who had shown himself infinite in grace and compassion.

V11: **A silly dove without sense** is one who is easily deceived and led into the prepared snare, a 'sucker'! Israel had been all too easily deceived by false prophets, idolatrous priests, and unscrupulous politicians. They had not thought things through (v9). No thoughtful people would have been deceived by such specious arguments.

They call to Egypt. They could have stayed within the dovecote of the divine protection, but instead they had called for aid from Egypt, where they had formerly been in bondage. Past experience should have warned them against that!

They go to Assyria, although the prophets had warned them that Assyria would be the Lord's rod of correction. They changed their allegiance from one to the other, but neither of these much sought-after allies could be trusted.

V12: Their designs to escape were likened by God to a bird flying into a fowler's net. Whatever they did, they would not escape. The nations are God's agents. His plans would be accomplished because he is the Lord of the nations and the director of all history.

According to what their congregation has heard. There is a difficulty here, and the NIV follows the Septuagint, assuming a poetic parallelism: **When I hear them flocking together I will catch them.** The NKJ reading emphasises that they had continually been warned of the consequences of their sinful folly, first by Moses (*Deut.* 28–29), and since that time by the prophets. The Lord had set before them the way of cursing and the way of blessing (*Deut.* 30:19), and they had chosen the former.

V13: They had fled from God, like foolish birds, deserting the nest which would have been the place of safety. As though it was not enough to forget God, they were now deliberately defying him. They had **transgressed**, rebelliously casting off God's law and his government.

Though I redeemed them. Their sin was aggravated by the fact that God had in love brought them out of the bondage of Egypt. The NIV renders this as the Lord's present desire to deliver them: 'I long to redeem them.'

Yet they have spoken lies against Me. They had done this in a number of ways:

a) They had pretended to worship God while giving allegiance to idols.

b) They ascribed to idols the mercies and provision they had enjoyed.

c) They had embraced idols as though God would not interest himself in their case.

d) They blamed God for not delivering them, when the real reason for all their distress was their own sin.

V14: The prophet Jeremiah later makes a similar complaint against Judah (see *Jer.* 3:10). He, too, speaks of a true turning to God, a turning with all their heart (*Jer.* 29:13, *Deut.* 4:29). It has been well said that no one is an atheist when in trouble, but men need to be clear about which God they are calling!

They wailed. Their cries were not of repentance, but more probably of self-pity, like a frustrated child going to his room, casting himself upon the bed and howling in a frenzy of anger, self-pity and despair. Calvin interprets: 'They are not touched with grief for having offended me, though they see by evident proofs that I am displeased with them: they regard not my favour or my displeasure, provided they enjoy plenty of wine and corn: this satisfies them, and it is all the same with them whether I am adverse or propitious to them.'

A slight amendment of the Hebrew would give 'they howled beside their altars', indicating their anguished idolatry.

They assemble together for grain and new wine. 'They came together only to seek the blessings of corn and new wine' (Matthew Henry). 'They gathered together in the house of their idols, so that they might have plenty to satisfy their appetite, instead of turning in repentance and faith to the true God' (Matthew Poole).

Some modern translations follow the Septuagint and a few Hebrew manuscripts to read **for the sake of grain and new wine they gash themselves**, indicating ritual extravagance usually associated with the prophets of Baal.

They rebel against Me. Whether by idol worship or empty ceremonial, they were in rebellion against God, a rebellion intensified by their pre-occupation with material things.

V15: In spite of his watching over them with tender fatherly care, they devised evil against him. They had accepted all the material benefits of the long and relatively prosperous reign of Jeroboam II without considering for a moment the hand from which those benefits had come. Instead they had used them to feed their false sense of security in their rebellion against the Lord.

V16: They return, *but* not to the Most High. Some suggest that this referred particularly to the reign of Jehu, when the worship of the Tyrian Baal was exterminated but there was no return to true worship of the Lord. Some older writers have suggested that Hoshea, the last king of Israel, gave liberty to the people to go to Jerusalem to worship, but even in this there was no real change of heart.

A treacherous bow is a weapon upon which the archer cannot depend, since the arrows deviate from the target or fall short. Some commentators take this to refer to their pretended worship of God. Others apply it to their vain political schemes.

The **princes** are specifically mentioned, since those who had special responsibility would experience special judgement (cf. 5:1).

The cursing of their tongue. Calvin takes this to refer to their pride, as they haughtily boasted of their strength and success. Poole understands it to be their outcry against God, his prophets and his providences. Some have suggested that it refers to their vaunted security and perverse defence of their idolatry. Still others have applied it to God's anger at what they say, which will bring them to the place of derision.

This *shall be* their derision in the land of Egypt. The reference may be to the derision of the Egyptians, who recently were supposed to be their allies but now regarded them with scorn. Or Egypt here could represent the place of bondage to which they would go.

FOR MEDITATION

1. Outline for the chapter: 'I would, but they would not!' (*Matt.* 23:37–39):

a) The *corruption of Israel* (v1).
b) The *cause of Israel's corruption* (v10).
c) The *course of Israel's corruption* (vv7, 8, 9, 11, 16).
d) The *consequence of Israel's corruption* (v13, hardened in sin; v16, overthrown and derided).

2. Whenever God in grace opened a door of mercy, Israel, as it were, kicked it shut by new expressions of rebellion. It is always sin which closes the door to mercy (*Isa.* 59:1–2). We must continually seek grace to go through the door, open to all who are 'poor in spirit' (*Matt.* 5:3). Our greatest problem is pride, and only the Holy Spirit can subdue the proud heart.

3. *They do not consider.* Pride causes spiritual blindness (*John* 9:39–41). We need to weigh carefully the awful darkness of the soul without Christ (*Eph.* 4:17–19). Is our pride worth such a price? Knowing this truth should fill us with patient concern for those who do not respond to our witness and drive us to prayer that God may open their eyes. An interesting illustration of prayer for spiritual illumination is found in 2 Kings 6:17.

4. Vv 3–13: Consider the things God hates (*Prov.* 6:16–19):
a) *Falsehood,* which includes all lying and hypocrisy. My whole Christian life is a lie if I profess but do not obey!
b) *Stealing,* which includes false weights and measures. This includes taking advantage with a firm's or the public's property, fiddling expense accounts, and any dishonest business. By gossip, it is possible to steal a person's good name. It is said that Absalom stole the hearts of the people of Israel from David by subtlety (*2 Sam.* 15:6), which is a warning against undermining someone's reputation falsely. And we should be very careful lest we rob God (*Mal.* 3:9–10).
c) *Adultery.* Sex is not for self-indulgence but for the glory of God and for self-giving. It should be a cause of concern for

Christians that it has become the number one subject for entertainment. The teaching of the Word of God is clear – sexual intercourse is intended to be within marriage and constitutes the 'one-flesh relationship' intended by God to exist between husband and wife. The man who puts away his wife without biblical cause commits adultery. Our world is becoming increasingly casual about this, and churches are becoming increasingly compromised by failure to maintain Christian standards. Whatever else we can do, Christians should, by example, demonstrate Christian standards by restraint before marriage and by faithfulness within it.

d) *Heavy drinking and debauchery.* The Scriptures indict these things as the expressions of overheated passions, yet our society creates clubs for this purpose and young people are put under much pressure to conform to this self-indulgence as a sign of adulthood (*Prov.* 23:29–35).

e) *Failure in separation.* The Israelites, who had cast aside God's standards to embrace those of the heathen, were now being threatened with the judgement of God. In our society some Christians encourage and embrace the values of the world, trying to look as much like men of the world as possible, and claim that this is the way to build bridges to the outsider. But we must face the truth, whether we like it or not, that our hearts are deceitful and prone to worldliness. We are inclined to shirk the way of self-discipline and find excuses for self-indulgence. The Lord Jesus put the need for separation and self-discipline uncompromisingly (*Luke* 14:26–27, 33). He will not tolerate lukewarmness (*Rev.* 3:14–21). We must ask ourselves whether our toleration is really compromise because we have no heart for the Christian warfare.

f) *Pride.* I may shudder at the boasting of the godless and yet be full of my own self-righteousness, taking pride in the soundness of my doctrine, my testimony, my Christian work or my giving. Am I too full of myself to be filled with the Holy Spirit?

As we review these things that God hates, we see an inescapable indictment of our society, and in some cases, of the church. We should remember that large numbers of people from other religions who have made their homes in our country regard what they see in our society as 'Christian standards'. Paul spoke of the name of God being blasphemed among the Gentiles because of the inconsistent behaviour of the Jews (*Rom.* 2:24). Today Christendom may be challenged as blaspheming the Lord's Name by its wilful neglect of Christian truth and moral standards. Have I prayed and behaved as I should in relation to this matter?

5. *The grey hairs* of spiritual decline. Many men and women anxiously look into the mirror to see whether grey hairs are appearing, and, when they do, they take steps to hide them. Are we so careful to watch for evidences of spiritual decline? Perhaps we need to look more carefully into the mirror of God's Word (*James* 1:22–25), and pray the prayer of Psalm 139:23–24, 'Search me, O God.' Sin and slackness creep into our lives all too easily. We need first to expose ourselves to the searching light of God's Word, which can discern the innermost thoughts and intents of the heart, and then seek the help of the Holy Spirit to bring us to repentance. Neglect is a terrible sin (*Heb.* 2:1–3, 12–13; 6:1–6; 10:16–21, 35–36).

6. Vv1–8: The prayer of John Calvin:

Grant, Almighty God, that, since thou hast once shone upon us by thy gospel, – O grant, that we may always be guided by this light, and so guided, that all our lusts may be restrained; and may the power of thy Spirit extinguish in us every sinful fervour, that we may not grow hot with our own perverse desires, but that all these things being subdued, we may gather new fervour daily, that we may breathe after thee more and more: nor let the coldness of our flesh ever take possession of us, but may we continually advance in the way of piety, until at length we come to that blessed rest to which thou invitest us, and which has been obtained for us by the blood of thy only-begotten Son, our Lord Jesus Christ. Amen.

7. V9: *He does not know it.* Consider well the example of Samson (*Judg.* 16:20). On every hand are strangers, ready to devour our strength without our being aware of it. The pursuing of worldly ambitions, over-indulgence in private hobbies, the influence of friends, can all preoccupy us and rob us of the time we need for that communion with God which restores spiritual strength. There is an old saying that 'unspiritual Saturday nights make for powerless Sunday mornings'. Self-indulgence may lie heavily upon our spirits like too much steak and kidney pudding on the stomach. 'One of the paradoxes of our time is that while few ages have borne more tragic evidences of sin, few ages have been less conscious of it' (H.C. Phillips). The self-confidence of twentieth-century man has made him almost impervious to the voice of conscience and his need of repentance towards God.

8. *A silly dove without sense.* Here are people without affection (*2 Tim.* 3:2–3), without conviction (*Eph.* 4:19, *Rom.* 1:32), and without understanding (*Eph.* 4:18). They are so full of self-love that they have no love for anyone else; so absorbed by it that they will do anything for their own immediate advantage; and so blinded by it that they never bother to analyse the consequences of their actions or look at their own faults. Such people are easily flattered and trapped. How does God see us?

9. V11: *They call to Egypt, they go to Assyria.* We need to recognise how prone we are to turn everywhere except to God, clutching at straws rather than anchoring in the Rock of Ages. We can make the prayer of Psalm 119:37 our own: 'Turn away my eyes from looking at worthless things.'

10. V13: *They transgressed against me though I redeemed them.* Their flagrant ingratitude is typical of fallen mankind. The person who goes to hell having heard the gospel has deliberately turned to spit on the face of the Redeemer, however intellectual and well versed in etiquette he may be! To reject Christ is the worst of all human sins (*Heb.* 6:4–8).

11. V13: *They have spoken lies against me.* The Israelites knew that the promises of God were true. Redemption was the basis of their national history and experience. Equally, they were shown by history to be liars, having entered into a covenant they had not kept. They had frequently expressed repentance, but they had not changed their ways. Rather than glorifying God for their deliverances, they had attributed these to themselves or to idols. They had worshipped with their lips while their hearts had remained far from God.

We should ask ourselves: Does my life suggest that I, too, am a liar? Is my religion an outward profession to catch the eye of others, or is it in singleness of heart, fearing the Lord? Do I claim to be God's child while showing little or nothing of his grace? Do I make promises and vows I do not keep? Do I pretend to repent, but continue in my sins and make excuses? Do I accept God's favours but attribute them to my own abilities or good luck?

12. V16: *They return but not to the most high.* Repentance is a gift of God (*2 Tim.* 2:25). It is possible to make a show of repentance and even to put right certain aspects of wrong behaviour, but no one can change his heart, except by a work of grace (*Jer.* 13:23). The Bible does not talk of a 'reformed heart', but of a 'new heart'. Our heart is like a deceitful bow which will always miss the mark, except for the miracle of re-generation. Whilst we can observe the forms of religion and seek to apply the edicts of morality, we cannot make ourselves

right with God. We need to fly to the Lord Jesus Christ! Unless he dwells within us, we are reprobate (*2 Cor.* 13:5). True repentance includes the acknowledgement of the painful truth that I cannot do it myself.

13. V13:Three aspects of sin are demonstrated: a) going astray, turning aside from God; b) a more aggravated attitude of rebellion; and c) the ultimate evidence of rejection, of speaking lies against God, that is, attributing to him things that are untrue and denying that he cares. This was the sin of the serpent himself (*Gen.* 3:3–5), and the man who commits it shows whose child he is.

14. If the Lord is to train, chasten and strengthen us, we need:
   a) an open ear to receive instruction (*Psa.* 40:6–8);
   b) a yielded heart to accept correction (*Psa.* 119:32, 59, 67, 71);
   c) a humble mind to accept help (*Matt.* 18:3).

15. Thinking of the Lord as *the pride of Israel*, I must ask 'In what shall I glory?' The Scriptures give some good answers.
   'In God we boast all day long' (*Psa.* 44:8).
   'Let him who glories glory in this, that he understands and knows Me, that I *am* the LORD, exercising lovingkindness, judgement, and righteousness in the earth' (*Jer.* 9:24).
   'God forbid that I should boast except in the cross of our Lord Jesus Christ' (*Gal.* 6:14).
   We may boast that only through the grace of God, by our Lord Jesus Christ, and not by works, we are saved (*Eph.* 2:8–9).

Chapter 8:1–14

'Set the Trumpet to Your Mouth'

V1: **The trumpet** is the instrument of warning (as in 5:8), and the renewed threat of God's judgement is a further call to repentance. The Lord has a tender heart to forgive, but he saves men *out* of sin, not *in* it. Divine forgiveness requires repentance; it is not a meritorious work, but an evidence of turning to God. Holy love cannot allow men to remain secure in their sins.

An eagle may refer to 'a vulture', as in RSV. This would be appropriate since the hovering vulture would represent imminent destruction. Calvin suggests that the eagle symbolises the speed with which the judgement would fall upon Israel; the eagle is swift in its descent on prey. Or the reference might be to the might and ferocity of Assyria. 2 Kings 15:9 tells of the Assyrian invasion during the reign of Pekah.

The house of the LORD often refers to the Jerusalem temple, but since the prophecy here is pointed against the Northern Kingdom, it may refer to that kingdom as God's household. They were still God's property, in spite of their rebellion.

Because. They had broken God's covenant and rebelled against his law. Like Esau of old, they had despised their inheritance. Though the covenant had been established by the grace of God, their enjoyment of it depended upon their obedience as a response to his love.

V2: In their deep distress they would cry out, pleading the ancient promises and pretending knowledge of God. But this was sheer hypocrisy, since their deeds denied their plea. This is not to be understood as referring to some future time of national repentance, but to their present hypocritical protestations, of which God has already given his estimate: they are like the morning cloud which soon disperses (6:4).

V3: They have cast off that which is good, and the enemy will pursue them.

V4: The nature of their sin is seen in two particulars: their independent appointment of kings and princes, and their idolatry. It is true that Ahijah had foretold that Jeroboam would become king (*1 Kings* 11:29–36), but there is no evidence that Israel sought God's guidance in the matter of his appointment (*1 Kings* 12:20). He led the kingdom into idolatry from the beginning with their full consent (*1 Kings* 12:28–30). The prophecy shows that God himself acted in bringing judgement on Rehoboam and Jerusalem. He promised to establish Jeroboam as an independent king, but upon the condition of obedience (*1 Kings* 11:38), which was never forthcoming.

This is an interesting example of how wilful men are found doing what God purposes without any intention or awareness of what they are doing. The same principle is seen in the death of Jesus at the hands of the Jewish authorities (*Acts* 2:23).

The later kings of Israel, after the death of Jeroboam II, were particularly upstart. Shallum, Menahem, Pekah, and Hoshea were all usurpers who came to the throne by violence.

We should remember, too, that the nation's demand for a king in Samuel's time was seen as an act of rebellion (*1 Sam.* 8:7–8).

Their silver and gold. The wealth which God had graciously provided to encourage them to repent and to walk with him was used to make idols. We are reminded of when Aaron and the people used the gold taken from the Egyptians to make a golden calf (*Exod.* 32:2–5).

That they might be cut off. Matthew Poole comments that 'by this they thought to establish themselves, but it will be quite contrary, these sins will be their ruin.'

V5: **Your calf is rejected.** Since there is no evidence of a calf image having been placed at Samaria, the city must here represent the whole Northern Kingdom. Israel had rejected the good (v3), and God rejects that which they had installed in his place!

My anger is aroused. The reality of the anger of the true God is contrasted with the futility of the idol. The idol will be consumed by the wrath of God as fire consumes wood. **Them** may refer to the calf idols at Dan and Bethel or to the whole people.

How long? Poole suggests God is answering the prophet's question, 'How long will your anger burn?'. The Lord replies, 'How long will it be before they are pure?' as though God himself were surprised at their hanging on to sin despite threats of impending ruin. This may be one way of saying that there would be no remission as long as there was no evidence of repentance.

V6: **For from Israel** *is* **even this.** Like the kings and princes (v4), the calf idols were also the product of Israel's fertile mind for rebellion. Made by men, they were plainly no deities. This would soon become evident, as they would be broken in pieces. The Hebrew word may mean either 'breaking in pieces' or 'consuming by fire'.

V7: Cause and effect is emphasised. When their sowing came to full fruition, they would reap a veritable whirlwind. This would not be the consequence of some divine caprice, but the outworking of divine moral principle. We should remember that we do not sow in expectation of a 'one for one' harvest; we expect an increase. The spiritual law parallels the natural. Calvin applies this to the sowing of the empty religious forms in the

Northern Kingdom. The idols were 'vanity' (wind), and the result would be devastating!

The second part of the verse says that nothing they did would prosper, and even if it did, aliens would consume it. The worthlessness of unconsecrated labour is vividly illustrated. Haggai later uses a different picture to teach a similar lesson (*Hag.* 1:6).

V8: Israel would be scattered among the nations like an unwanted piece of pottery discarded by the potter. Jeremiah later broke a potter's vessel to demonstrate the judgement of God upon Judah. We are reminded that the potter has the right to do as he wills with the vessels he makes (*Rom.* 9:21; cf. *Jer.* 18:4). This verse may also suggest that the nations to whom they ran for protection would find no pleasure in them either.

V9 refers to Israel's attempt to purchase Assyrian favour (cf. *Hos.* 7:9, 11, *2 Kings* 15:19).

A wild donkey gives a picture of untamed lust. There is a play on the name 'Ephraim' and 'wild ass'.

Alone by itself, exposed to the threat of the Assyrian lion, without any source of help. They had turned away from God, who would have sustained them.

Ephraim has hired lovers. By their self-will and perverseness they had cut themselves off. Without reliable friends or allies, they must now try to purchase 'lovers' and buy themselves friends. This indicates the folly of their political alliances.

V10: In doing this they had thought to secure themselves from the threats made by the prophets, but the Lord will gather them. As Matthew Henry puts it: 'What they had provided for their safety shall but make them easier prey to their enemies. There is no fence against the judgements of God.' Calvin comments that this may be understood as a word of mercy: God will gather them to preserve them that they may grieve a little.

Sorrow a little may be translated 'begin to waste away' (NIV). The **burden** may be the heavy tribute exacted by Assyria (NIV: 'under the oppression of the mighty king').

V11: **Many altars for sin** refers to the many altars in the Northern Kingdom, in opposition to the true altar in Jerusalem. These would be the ground of God's judgement upon them as well as the occasion of further sin, as God delivered them over to the blindness of heart symbolised by these altars.

V12: The law of God had been given particularly to the nation Israel, with great and detailed care, a privilege not granted to other peoples (*Rom.* 3:1–2; 9:4). But they had regarded it as something alien. What should have been a source of delight was instead regarded with hostility. A modern parallel is seen in our own society's rejection of the moral law of God. It should be a source of delight to the believer (*Psa.* 119:97), though it is an offence to the ungodly (cf. *Rom.* 7:8–11, 22).

V13: The first part of the verse may be understood in two ways:

a) They continued to offer the sacrifices according to the law, and ate the meat, which suggested communion with God; but the Lord would not accept sacrifices from such sinful hands.

b) Their only interest was in eating the meat of the sacrifices. Their concern was with 'feeding their faces'.

Either way, the Lord would not accept such sacrifices!

The reference to Egypt may be taken literally, or it may suggest a return to bitter bondage such as they had experienced in Egypt (cf. *Deut.* 28:68, *Hos.* 9:6).

V14: **Israel has forgotten his Maker** (cf. *Deut.* 32:15, 18). The Lord was their maker in a special way because his grace had made them the nation they became. The language was not only a reminder of their special relationship with God, made possible by his grace alone, but also of the many warnings they had received from the time of Moses against the sins into which they had fallen.

Temples (NKJ); **palaces** (NIV). Both are possible. They had built temples to their idols to replace the true temple at Jerusalem ordained by God himself. They had also built palaces for themselves and their apostate monarchy. Archaeology suggests that the capital of the Northern Kingdom, Samaria, was at this time a city of great wealth (*Amos* 6:1, 4). The idea of temples also shows that although Israel had forsaken the true God, the nation was more religious than ever.

Judah's **fortified cities** (cf. *2 Chron.* 26:10–15; 27:7). Uzziah and Jotham both built extensive fortifications. These testify that Judah's trust too was in the 'arm of the flesh' rather than in the Lord, as is later indicated by Jeremiah (*Jer.* 17:5–7).

End of verse 14, **palaces** (NKJ); **fortresses** (NIV). We are told of the occupation of many fortified cities by Sennacherib during his invasion of Judah (*2 Kings* 18:13–15).

FOR MEDITATION

1. Reflections on the chapter:
   a) The *substitutes.* Idols were put in the place of God (vv4–5).
   b) The *society.* Priorities were false, the wrong things trusted and sought after (vv9–10).
   c) The *sacrifices.* Worship was wrongly motivated (vv11–13).

2. Thoughts on the chapter:
   a) *What they had spurned:*
      • They had forgotten God (v14).
      • They had spurned his law (v12). The warnings of the book of Deuteronomy had been forgotten (*Deut.* 8; 28–30).

b) *How?*
  • They had given outward assent without inward worship (vv2–3).
  • They had followed the pattern of the world around them (v4).
  • They had failed in separation to God (v9).

c) *What they had served:*
  • Idols (vv4–5).
  • Self: their personal desires and lusts (v13).
  • Materialism (v14).
  • Allies among the nations (vv9–10).

d) *What they had sown:*
  • The wind (v7; cf. *Eccles.* 1:7, *Psa.* 127:1–2).

e) *What they would reap:*
  • The whirlwind! God's Word points to a better sowing (*Psa.* 126:5–6, *Gal.* 6:8).

3. The preacher may be seen as a watchman (v1; cf. *Ezek.* 3: 16–21). Though the Lord Jesus Christ was all tenderness, he reminded those who heard him that their situation was one of 'repent or perish' (*Luke* 13:1–5, *Matt.* 23:37–39).

4. V2: *My God, we know You.* Here we are warned against false and presumptuous confidence. Departure from God does not mean the forsaking of all religion. In hypocrisy and spiritual blindness we can still use all the correct forms and the most beautiful words. Man-centred and humanly devised religion may be emotionally moving and intellectually satisfying.

Distress may cause us to cry out to God most eloquently, but even that is not necessarily true repentance. We have the example of Saul (*1 Sam.* 15:24–30). The motive may be self-pity rather than the acknowledgement of our sin in the sight of God, the grievous nature of our covenant breaking before him, and our dishonouring of his holy name. We may be attempting to earn merit rather than adoring the abundance of his grace. We may be more concerned about our standing in the sight of the world than the glory of his name.

5. These solemn warnings are an act of grace. God might have destroyed them right away! We need to recapture the sense of the awfulness of the divine judgement and its imminence. The Lord Jesus did not mince matters on this score. Men deserve hell, and apart from the grace of God they have no better destiny in view (*Mark* 9:42–48).

6. V3 reminds us of the folly of Israel's rebellion. It was 'the casting off of what was good'. We are often no better when we give way to the instinct for independence, which leads us into bondage to some man-made idol, whether material or intellectual, whether it be an '-osophy' or an '-ology'. Even within the church establishment, we are prone to live and to legislate without the authority of the Word of God. How many matters are being dealt with today without regard for the teaching of Scripture? Calvin said that man's mind was a veritable idol factory.

7. V4: Are we guilty of committing our lives to other rulers? Does the Lord Jesus alone reign? Remember the reflection attributed to Cardinal Wolsey: ' If only I had served my God as faithfully as I have served my king.' Let us make the prayer of William Cowper our own:

> *The dearest idol I have known,*
> *What e'er that idol be,*
> *Help me to tear it from thy throne,*
> *And worship only thee.*

8. V7 warns us against forgetting that the inevitable result of sowing is multiplication. The seeds of sins and self-will yield a

final harvest of disaster, but sowing in the Spirit will yield the fruits of everlasting life. When we consider the disintegration of families and the present disruption of society, we must surely begin to be aware that this is the consequence of the 'new morality' and the national turn away from God. Whatever the politicians and theorists promise, repentance towards God is the only way forward to a 'new life'.

9. V9: The *wild ass* does not appreciate the hand that feeds it. It seeks only the gratification of its animal desires. It travels alone, and at length it dies alone, prey to cruel marauders. Do not be a wild ass! There is a lion about (*1 Pet.* 5:8)! We have been created in the image of God for better things, and though we are now fallen away from God, in mercy he calls us to be 'made new' (*Eph.* 4:22–24).

10. V12: The *law of God* is part of the covenant of grace. We are not saved by keeping the law, but attention to it will, under the influence of the Spirit of God, bring conviction of sin and lead us to Christ. When we have believed, the Spirit bears witness that these words are good and true and faithful (*Psa.* 19:7–10; 119:75, 138, 140, 160, 165). God's law should be our delight as it brings conviction of sin, leads us to the Lord Jesus Christ as our Redeemer, and assists our daily walk with him (*1 John* 5:2–3).

Ask: Does God's verdict upon Israel apply to me in any way? Are there spiritual laws to which the Holy Spirit is bearing witness but from which I am turning away and counting them 'strange'? Do I have a new heart which finds obedience a delight (*Ezek.* 36.27)?

11. V13 challenges us that religious forms may continue to be observed while the Lord has been forgotten. Men may find satisfaction in beautiful buildings, poetic worship, pleasurable

and exciting music, whether classical or modern. They may find some emotional fulfilment. They may enjoy the companionship of like minds and attain religious and moral standards, yet without ever seeking the true God. We must continually examine ourselves as to whether we are doing any more than going through the motions (see *Hos.* 6:6, *Mic.* 6: 6–8, *1 Cor.* 11:28, *2 Cor.* 13:5).

12. The final verse of the chapter is a timely comment on contemporary self-sufficiency and self-indulgence, as well as a warning concerning the end-product of such living.

Chapter 9:1–9

The Threat of Captivity

V1: The opening words may suggest that the people had some reason to rejoice at this time. The situation may be the special prosperity of the reign of Jeroboam II, or the peace contract made by Menahem with Assyria (*2 Kings* 15:19–20). Doubtless the people thought this would bring them safety, rather after the manner of Mr Chamberlain's 'piece of paper' on the eve of the Second World War. Whatever the reason for their optimism, God tells them that there is no good reason for it in the light of the judgement he had decreed.

Like *other* peoples, after their manner, with the same kinds of celebrations and festivals with their pagan immoralities. Calvin suggests that though God might pardon other nations, he would punish Israel as inexcusable, so they had no cause for joy.

The theme of their harlotry is taken up again. The **threshing floor** refers to the pagan rites connected with the fertility cults. Jeremiah later seems to refer to the same practices in Judah (*Jer.* 44:17–18).

V2: The nation would be deprived of its prosperity so that they might see the vanity of their false gods, as had been threatened before (2:4–12). Calvin illustrates the point: 'Stripes do no good, all warnings are slighted; but when the boy who loves excess sees that bread is denied him, he finds out that his father's displeasure ought to be feared. Thus God corrects men addicted to excessive indulgence.'

V3: Their fate will be the opposite of prosperity: they are warned here of captivity. Probably Egypt is intended symbolically (as in 8:13)as a place of captivity and bondage.

Eat unclean *things* in Assyria. This states clearly the place of their captivity. Further, they will lose their distinctiveness as God's people by being compelled to eat unclean meats, contrary to the law of Moses.

V4: The **wine *offerings*** were originally appointed with the morning and evening sacrifices to symbolise joy and fruitfulness in the land which was God's gift to them. Because they would be captives in a strange land, these would now cease.

Their sacrifices would not be pleasing to God, and they would take no pleasure in them (cf. *Amos* 5:21). Some sacrifices spoke of atonement for sin, some of dedication, others of fellowship; but all were vain and empty because of their sinfulness. The Lord would not honour them.

The bread of mourners. The sacrificial meals which had once been occasions of joyous fellowship with God would now be occasions of sorrow, because the people would be far away from their own land and would not be able to offer their first-fruits or observe their daily thanksgiving. All would be ceremonially unclean (*Num.* 19:22, *Deut.* 26:14). The remembrance of God would no longer bring delight but regret, because the hand of his judgement was upon them.

For their bread *shall be* for their *own* life. Their bread will serve the sole purpose of keeping them alive. Some commentators understand: 'let them serve themselves and their stomachs with bread, and no more offer it to God, for they cannot consecrate to God their bread when they themselves are unclean.' Calvin prefers the sense that God has excluded his ungodly people from himself as by an interdict, though in their hypocrisy they would boldly present themselves before him.

V5: The prophet pictures the perplexity of the people in the midst of their bondage on the occasions of their great religious festivals. They would be compelled to acknowledge the grace and favour of the Lord in former days, celebrated by those festivals. And they would be compelled to admit that through sin they had forfeited these blessings.

V6: **For indeed they are gone because of destruction**. There is some doubt about the Hebrew. The NIV renders this phrase: 'even if they escape destruction', and the RSV offers: 'they are going to Assyria'. The sense is clear enough that there is no way of escape.

Egypt shall gather them up: Memphis shall bury them. There is a striking play on the Hebrew words 'gather' and 'bury' (*kober* and *kobets*). Memphis had one of the largest burial grounds in Egypt. Brushwood was 'gathered' into a bundle for the fire. This may depict survivors fleeing in the opposite direction from the advancing Assyrian army. But since 11:5 emphatically states that Israel will not return to Egypt, it may be better to read this reference to Egypt symbolically. Perhaps some people in the Northern Kingdom did escape to Egypt. Some of the southern exiles fled there at a later date (*2 Kings* 25:26), and Jeremiah was eventually taken there (*Jer.* 42–43). Memphis was situated on the Nile about fifteen miles from the apex of the delta. It was the capital of the Old Kingdom and remained important until the time of Alexander the Great.

Valuables of silver may refer to the treasure cities or to the idols. **Thorns** may suggest the curse of God upon them (*Gen.* 3:18). **Tents** could refer either to the dwellings of the people or to the temples of their gods. The depopulation of the country is in view.

V7: These disasters are seen as a reckoning. The Jews were under the mistaken impression that the 'day of the Lord' would be a day of blessing, but they were about to see that the Lord could visit them in wrath (cf. *Amos* 5:18–20).

The prophet *is* a fool. The phrase has been explained in various ways:

a) Hosea is speaking of the true prophet, who would be beside himself with sorrow at the stubborn nature of the people's sin and the awfulness of the divine judgement upon it.

b) The prophet is being derided by the people for his pessimistic message. In their immediate prosperity it seemed inconceivable that such disasters could befall them.

c) Hosea may be speaking of the false prophets and pretended wise men with their glib talk of prosperity. These would be shown up as fools by the events of the judgement. So Calvin suggests that 'all Israel will know in that day, that the prophets to whom they have been listening have been deceived'.

V8: Again, various interpretations have been offered. The prophet sent by God is the true watchman (cf. *Ezek.* 3:17), but there is hostility to him on every hand.

Calvin offers the sense that the office of the prophet was from God, and he could effectively discharge his ministry only as connected with him; but these men, bearing such an exalted name and title, were nothing more than the snare of a fowler.

Poole sees the true prophet, sent by God, contrasted with the false prophet upon whom the people doted and depended, but whose predictions were a snare and who were hated by God for their foul deceptions.

The overall meaning is clear, however, that Israel was on the road to ruin ensnared by false prophets.

V9: **They are deeply corrupted.** The depravity of Israel is compared to that revealed at Gibeah (*Judg.* 19). (Another reference to this appears in 10:9). It had first appeared that the tribe of Benjamin would triumph in spite of their sinful perverseness, but the judgement of God came upon them at last. So here, Israel's gross perverseness in the sight of God would not go unpunished. Contrast with this the wonder of the new covenant promise that sin will be remembered no more (*Jer.* 31:34).

FOR MEDITATION

1. In days of prosperity and ease, it is important to search our hearts before God, lest we live in the same false security that Israel did. The human heart may cause us to be lulled into the false assumption that temporary prosperity is a sign of divine favour. Instead we need to remember that God, the Father of lights, with whom there is no variation or shadow of change, is the giver of every good and perfect gift (*James* 1:17). He may well be dealing with us in mercy, calling us back to himself by kindness and patience.

2. 'We may learn to prize spiritual bread, by being made to feel the want of it' (Matthew Henry).

3. Jesus reminds us of the impermanence of earthly riches (*Matt.* 6:19–21). Hosea teaches the same lesson as he foretells how the treasures and glorious temples will lie desolate among weeds and thorns. Many silent mounds in the Middle East bear testimony to this truth from God's Word. Material things, built up by great effort and at great cost, are easily undermined and overthrown. One is reminded of the parable of the rich fool (*Luke* 12:16–20). The only sure foundation is the Word of the Lord (*Matt.* 7:24–27).

4. V8: The true prophet may be regarded as crazy and be greatly despised, but he is God's watchman. Through the centuries faithful men have undergone much abuse for their faithfulness to the Word of God. The stand for truth may be costly!

The Lord sees the false prophet as foolish, even though men may dote on them and honour them. But events will finally prove their arguments false. Ask: Am I more concerned about how I stand in the eyes of men than in the sight of God? Am I prepared to be 'a fool for Christ's sake', or shall I be one of those who at the last will be shown to be a fool before God?

5. A comment from Calvin about false prophets: 'These prophets live not in caves nor traverse the public roads, but they occupy a place in the temple of God; so that of the sacred temple of God they make a brothel for the impostures of Satan.'

The Son of Man had no place to lay his head (*Luke* 9:62). The loyal prophets often faced much persecution. They were sometimes compelled to be fugitives, not infrequently imprisoned, and sometimes put to death (*2 Kings* 19:14). By contrast, the false prophets seem to have stood high in the favour of the national leaders. They often did not mix with the common people but gave themselves airs and accepted the favours of reprobate princes.

The Lord warned his disciples to beware when everyone spoke well of them (*Luke* 6:26). The false prophets were often highly honoured by the apostate church of the day. In our own day, ecclesiastical favours are not necessarily evidence of great spirituality, though spiritual men have at times attained high office. But we also see that men who deny the very fundamentals of the faith can receive great acclaim as theologians and biblical scholars.

The true believer will not concern himself with the favours and flatteries of the world, and messengers of God should not expect an easy time. It is important only to be one who is approved to God, who does not need to be ashamed, and who rightly divides the Word of truth' (*2 Tim.* 2:15). Think well on this before accepting any call to ministry!

6. The reference to Gibeah reminds us that the corruption of the human heart does not change with the passing generations. Genesis 6:5 – 'the wickedness of man *was* great in the earth, and every intent of the thoughts of his heart *was* only evil continually' – is still true today. The mode of sinning may change, but the iniquity of the heart does not. The main sins of Gibeah were sex, violence, and rabid tribalism. All of these have a very contemporary ring; the Bible is up to date. But it not only diagnoses the problem accurately. It also has the final answer, in the Lord Jesus Christ.

Chapter 9:10–17

'The Withering Away of Israel'

V10: **Grapes in the wilderness** were greatly prized and treasured. God found 'Jacob' in the wilderness (*Deut.* 32:10–12). Here is a picture in human terms of the potential God saw in Jacob and his delight in choosing this people. As the traveller in the wilderness rejoices when he comes upon an oasis with luscious fruit, so God took delight in the early response of Israel to his grace – though God had a deeper awareness of the nature of the hearts of the people and their essential sinfulness (*Deut.* 8:10–19; 9:6). Any potential was not of their merit, but by the working of his grace.

But **they went to Baal Peor.** The early promise was soon clouded by the sombre shades of sin as they turned aside to commit adultery with the daughters of Moab, falling into blatant sin and apostasy (*Num.* 25:1–5).

And separated themselves to *that* shame (see 4:7). It is suggested that the Hebrew *bosheth* ('shame') was sometimes used at this time to refer to the Baals. Instead of becoming a royal priesthood separated to God (*Exod.* 19:5–6) they had dedicated themselves to the Baals and become an abomination like the object they loved. So Calvin interprets: 'As Baal Peor is the highest abomination to me, so the people became to me equally abominable.'

V11: **Their glory shall fly away like a bird.** Some suggest that 'glory' here refers to their children. Calvin accepts this sense but does not confine the meaning here to offspring. It includes the whole condition of the nation and the prosperity granted to them by God. Remember that the name 'Ephraim' means 'double fruit'.

Fly away like a bird may express a sudden and unexpected disappearance. It contrasts with the divine constancy, which is compared with a parent eagle (*Deut.* 32:10–12).

No birth, no pregnancy, and no conception. The threat found in Deuteronomy 32:23–25 would be fulfilled. Some children would die as soon as they were born, and others would die by miscarriage. Some women would be barren. The religious prostitution carried on at the shrines of the false gods was thought to bring fertility; but instead, the judgement of God would condemn these idolaters to sterility.

V12: When children were brought into the world, the judgement of God would be upon them and their hope would be cut off. Children who did survive would not reach adulthood. It is surely woe to people when the Lord departs from them. This is indeed 'Ichabod' (*1 Sam.* 4:21) – the glory has departed! When the glory of the presence of God departs from his chosen people, their glory in every other way also departs.

V13: **I saw Ephraim like Tyre.** The verse is difficult, and commentators deal with it in a variety of ways:

Some, like the RSV, give up the Hebrew as too uncertain and follow the Greek Septuagint, which reads 'Ephraim's sons are, as I have seen, destined for the prey: Ephraim must lead forth his sons to slaughter.'

But many make an effort to do justice to the Hebrew. Some modern commentators point out that the Hebrew word which makes reference to Tyre is found in late Hebrew for a 'fir tree', and Ephraim is compared to 'a fir tree in a meadow'.

Calvin suggests that Ephraim was like a tree planted in Tyre, and interprets: 'Though the Israelites had been hitherto brought up in my bosom, and though I have kindly given them all kinds of blessings, and though they have been like tender trees, yet their condition hereafter shall be entirely different.'

The RV and Keil's commentary see the beauty of Israel compared to ancient Tyre, which was thought of as a place of great beauty (*Ezek.* 28:13).

The intent of the Hebrew seems to be that the great beauty and fruitfulness of Ephraim will be ruined by slaughter (or 'the slaughterer'), which is the sense given by the NKJ and NIV. This is an interesting example of how the sense of the most perplexing Old Testament texts can usually be understood without recourse to extensive amendment of the Hebrew.

V14: The sense is well given by Calvin: 'The prophet speaks – Lord I would gladly intercede for this people: what is it then that I should chiefly desire for them? Doubtless my chief wish, in their miserable condition, is that thou wouldst give them a killing womb and dry breasts, that is, that none may be born of them.' Matthew Poole sees this as the prayer of the prophet, that God would give them barrenness rather than the awful judgement of slaughter, like David in 2 Samuel 24, preferring that the people should fall into the hands of the Lord, rather than be given over to the punitive agency of men. Give them what thou art about to give!

V15: The idolatrous shrine at Gilgal embodied all the evil that marked Israel's history (see again 4:15). **From My house** is usually taken in this context to refer to the land of promise, the language being typical of the disowning of a son.

I will love them no more. Calvin gives the sense: 'I will not continue my love towards them, for I will now really show that I am angry with them, as I see that I have done nothing by my forbearance, which they do in a manner laugh to scorn.' He shows how God accommodates his language to human thought forms. Some expositors have understood that the Lord is threatening to withdraw the temporal tokens of his mercy, but Hosea has already shown (1:9) that something far more drastic is intended. What is said is the most dreadful phrase which can ever be spoken against a people, that God should 'cast them away'. But the Bible indicates that persistent sin can lead to such an end. In Romans 1:22–32, the phrase 'God gave them up' is repeated, and in the letter to the Hebrews, this possibility is set before the readers to call them back from ruin before it is too late.

All their princes *are* rebellious. The king and princes of the Northern Kingdom were seen as apostate from the time of its institution. There was no evidence of a remnant of grace among them, and that in spite of the ministries of Elijah and Elisha in their midst. This shows how great the patience of God, that he should bear with such people and grant them such blessings for so many generations. It puts into perspective, too, our measurement of the success of the preacher of the Word. Great prophets were sent to the Northern Kingdom who saw little fruit for their labours yet were faithful to their task. We cannot measure faithfulness by apparent results!

V16: This (as v11) reflects the meaning of 'Ephraim' as 'doubly fruitful'. The nation, potentially so fruitful, would be barren.

V17: **My God.** The prophet affirms his confidence in God, yet he knows that all their troubles have come from his hand. He has cast them off because they did not listen. We should compare the words of Jesus (*Matt.* 23:37–39) and be warned against such abuse of his grace.

They shall be wanderers. They will be like the children of Cain (*Gen.* 4:4). In less than fifty years all that Hosea prophesied was fulfilled, and today, more than 2,500 years later, they are still wanderers among the nations. Truly, the fear of the Lord is the beginning of wisdom (*Prov.* 1:7). The awesomeness of the prospect of his righteous wrath should drive us into the arms of his love!

FOR MEDITATION

1. Themes in chapter 9:
   a) The *iniquity of the nation's heart.*
   b) The *intensity of the prophet's grief.*
   c) The *ingratitude of Israel's rebellion.*
   d) The *inevitability of God's judgement.*

2. V10: All too often good beginnings give way to bad endings. Early days are often rich with promise of fruitful service and undivided love. Then people become ensnared by what the Apostle John calls 'loving the world' (*1 John* 2:15). How we need to heed the warnings of Scripture to lay aside every weight and keep our eyes fixed on the Lord Jesus (*Heb.* 12:1–3).

3. V10: The story of Baal Peor (*Num.* 22–25, 31) contains solemn warnings. The prophet Balaam was summoned to curse Israel, but found that because of the spirit of prophecy within him he could not restrain the pronouncement of the blessing God had purposed for them. Balak, the king of Moab, offered rich rewards if Balaam could find some way of overthrowing this people whom God had purposed to bless and who constituted a danger to him. Balaam's plan was to use the women of Moab to ensnare the men of Israel (*Num.* 31:16); the phrase 'the counsel of Balaam' became a proverb to speak of the appeal of sensuality to draw them away from God.

   In this story we are warned of the subtlety and perseverance of the enemies of God's people. The enemies are masterminded by Satan himself, the immensely powerful arch-enemy. Yet even he is subject to the authority of God and will finally be defeated on the behalf of believers by our glorious captain, the Lord Jesus Christ.

We are reminded of the frailty of our human nature. None of us is without an Achilles' heel in relation to the love of the world.

We see the appeal of false religion to our fallen humanity. Many religious people desire to share the end of the righteous (*Num.* 23:10) but are drawn away by the prospect of material blessing. To die the death of the righteous we must be identified now with the cross of the Lord Jesus, so that we may be partakers in his resurrection (*2 Cor.* 4:10–11). But to know the power of his resurrection, we must accept the 'fellowship of his sufferings' (*Phil.* 3:10).

The extent of the vengeance exacted (*Num.* 25:5; 31:7) should teach the need for an uncompromising attitude to anything that might pollute the faith. The Jews had been very clearly instructed that the inhabitants of the land were to be driven out, and their failure to do this may be seen as the seed of their later apostasy. Jesus expresses the same uncompromising attitude (*Matt.* 5:27–30, *Luke* 14:25–35).

In spite of all human efforts, the purposes of God cannot be frustrated: a warning to the ungodly but a word of encouragement to the embattled believer.

4. V10: *The firstfruits on the fig tree.* We observe that God's people are called to fruitfulness (*John* 15:1–5), but turning away from God leads first to barrenness and ultimately to destruction (*Luke* 13:6–9, *Jer.* 17:5–7). We must honestly ask ourselves, What fruit should the church of Jesus Christ be bearing? What is our fruit? What is our passion? Years ago, G Campbell Morgan wrote: 'The church today is cursed with fungus growths, all sorts of institutions, until one hears the constant click of the machinery, and then when we look for fruit, the supreme

question is "What is the fruit?" Is it that of the divine intention or that of our selfishness?'[1]

The Scriptures suggest a fourfold fruitfulness:
Spiritual gifts to strengthen believers (*Rom.* 1:11–13);
Christian character: the fruit of the Spirit (*Gal.* 5:22–23);
Good works (*Col.* 1:10);
Souls won to Christ (*Prov.* 11:30).

5. V10: *They became an abomination like the thing they loved.* There is a principle that we become like the things we love: so we must guard our hearts with all diligence (*Prov.* 4:23). The reaction of our young people to the 'idols' of the day, whether in sport or the arts, should not be a matter of indifference to Christian parents. Watchful care and prayerful instruction are needed. When Moses communed with God on the mountain, he came to reflect something of the divine glory. In the same way, the Christian is to reflect the glory of Christ (*2 Cor.* 3:18). Since we become like the things we love, we should set our hearts on the Lord Jesus Christ (*Col.* 3:1).

6. V13: *Ephraim planted in a pleasant place.* We ought to review continually the mercies of God towards us, particularly in these days when people seem so quick to complain about hard circumstances. The Christian is reminded of all the glorious potential in the Lord's planting (*Isa.* 58:11, *Jer.* 17:8). The Lord even promises to transform the desert into a pool (*Isa.* 35:7). Truly God plants his people in a pleasant place when he establishes us 'in Christ' (*Eph.* 1:3–10).

7. V15: Gilgal is a picture of religion gone sour. It was at first a place of consecration; then it became a place of self-assertion, when Saul was confirmed there as king. At last it became a place

[1] In *Hosea, the Heart and Holiness of God* (London: Marshall, Morgan & Scott, 1948), p.93.

of idolatry. When self ascends the throne of our life, it is not long before all kinds of lesser idols begin to populate the temple.

8. V17: *My God will cast them away.* God does not desire that anyone should perish (*Ezek.* 18:23,32, *1 Tim.* 2:4, *2 Pet.* 3:9).

He commands repentance (*Ezek.* 18:4, 23, 30–32, *Hos.* 10:12, *Luke* 13:5, *Acts* 17:30).

In his patience, he restrains judgement to give time to repent (*Mic.* 7:18, *2 Pet.* 3:9).

But he judges those who do not heed the call of mercy (*Matt.* 23:37–39, *John* 5:40).

The awfulness of being 'cast off by God' is mirrored in the sufferings of the Lord Jesus Christ upon the cross (*Matt.* 27:46, *Psa.* 22:1). We need to pray the prayer of David and seek God's restoring work in our soul (*Psa.* 51:10). It is only as the Lord works in our hearts that we can walk in his ways (*Psa.* 119:32).

Chapter 10:1–10

'A Twig on the Water!'

V1: The **vine** is a frequent symbol for Israel (cf. *Psa.* 80:8, *Jer.* 2:21). The Lord Jesus Christ used it as a symbol of his relationship with his church (*John* 15:1–5), a much more intimate relationship than that shown in the Old Testament. The symbol of the vineyard is used (*Isa.* 5:1–7, *Matt.* 21:23).

Israel empties *his* vine. An adjective is translated as a verb in the NKJ. The adjective is probably best translated literally as 'running', so either 'spreading' or 'luxuriant' is satisfactory; the NIV has 'spreading vine'.

A very similar word means 'empty', which is the sense given in the AV (and NKJ). Calvin speaks of Israel as 'a robbed vine', and Poole of 'a vine wasted and spoiled'.

Most modern translators understand the phrase to refer to Israel's being richly blessed with every kind of material blessing. Some interpreters suggest that it means the abundance of Israel's religious profession. The parable of the vineyard (*Isa.* 5), depicts the great care bestowed by God on his vineyard.

He brings forth fruit for himself. Some have read this as a question, giving the meaning that Israel is so plundered that no restoration could be expected. Calvin prefers the sense (which he regards as historically confirmed) that after the chastisement when they gathered new strength, they would continue in their selfish ways, so that nothing was accomplished by the Lord's moderating of the judgement. Poole suggests: 'Whatever fruit was brought forth by its remaining strength was not brought forth to God . . . but for themselves, for their own use.' Some modern translators omit 'for himself', but retaining the reflexive emphasises that Israel's fruitfulness was self-centred and not for the Lord. The translation is possible but not conclusive.

According to the multitude of his fruit. The fruitfulness which should have glorified God, instead gave rise to more idolatry. In the reign of Jeroboam II, Israel enjoyed great prosperity, but this was a time of increasing idolatry and its attendant evils (see 2:5).

Altars refer either to those dedicated to the heathen deities, or to the altars where debased worship of the Lord was conducted.

Sacred pillars. The Hebrew *massebah* refers to the standing stones beside the altars which were an essential part of the worship of the heathen cults.

V2: **Their heart is divided.** The Hebrew is *shalaq*, meaning 'smooth' or 'slippery'. Their deceitful and insincere worship is in view. A double-minded man is unstable in all his ways (*James* 1:18). The word was also used of the stones with which they cast lots and may represent the way the nation was 'dicing with God', playing him off against other gods and their foreign allies. God is not satisfied with such half-hearted allegiance.

Now they are held guilty. The Hebrew *ashem,* 'guilt', reminds us that sin is not weakness for which sympathy is to be shown, but crime against God, which requires punishment. All the emblems of false worship would be broken down, showing their complete vanity. This is God's action, demonstrating that he is the sovereign Lord over all.

V3: **We have no king.** This seems to suggest unbelieving rebellious despair. They had first rejected God as king when the nation had requested Samuel for a king (*1 Sam.* 8:5). But this may be a prophecy of the situation arising soon after the death of Jeroboam II, when three men occupied the throne in little more than a year. Calvin comments that so long as they had a king among them, they thought they were safe from every harm. But the day would come when they would be constrained to admit that they had no king because they had not feared God. Some read the statement absolutely, others take it in the sense of 'no king worth the name'.

And as for a king. They would be brought to realise that their kings would not profit them at all.

V4: This may be an explanation of the 'divided heart' of the people (v2), or it may refer to the failure of their kings, whose promises and covenants could not be relied upon.

Judgement (NKJ) might refer to the judgements of God, which would be as destructive as a poisoned plant. The NIV has 'lawsuits', referring to perverted justice and its poisoning effect on society. This may be the more likely sense here, in the light of Amos 5:7 and 6:12, which also speak of perverted justice.

V5: The inhabitants of Samaria would fear for their calf, whose destruction would symbolise the downfall of the nation. The plural feminine form is used here, and Leon Wood suggests that 'calf-hood' may be intended, to refer to the whole perverse system. It has also been suggested that a sarcastic reference may be intended to the female deities so typical of Baal worship.

Beth Aven, 'House of shame', substituted for Bethel (as in 4:15), expresses contempt for what Bethel, the original home of the entire perverse cult, has become. The calf there was the prototype of many all over the kingdom.

Priests. The word *hemarim* is used elsewhere in reference to idolatrous priests (*2 Kings* 23:5, *Zeph.* 1:4). God had disowned this priesthood of Israel: they were not his.

Theodore Laetsch suggests that this may refer to some ritual dance like that by the prophets of Baal in Elijah's contest with them at Mount Carmel (*1 Kings* 18:26); or it could be an expression of extreme sorrow by both priests and people.

The last part of verse 5 is difficult. The NIV expresses the sorrow of those who had formerly rejoiced over its splendour; the NKJ hints at the former day when the glory departed from Israel because the ark had been captured. There is no glory in false religion.

Glory or **splendour.** *Kabod* means 'weight', and from this is derived the idea of 'worth'. In the Old Testament it often refers to the visible presence of God (*2 Chron.* 7:1). Applied to the idol, it may mean the magnificence of the image in the temple or the imagined power of the god, in the same way that 'the glory' was the evidence to Israel of God's presence and power.

V6: The image would be carried away as a present to the king of Assyria (5:13), indicating its powerlessness to save. Calvin suggests that the idol may be broken up and its precious metal used as a bribe in an attempt to secure peace. The Northern Kingdom, filled with shame, would at last learn the futility of setting up a dumb idol as the protector of the nation. For a long time they had worshipped this 'shame', and now they would experience the fruit of their shameful worship.

Counsel could be the first setting up of the calf worship at Bethel under Jeroboam I, or it might be the policy of the kings who succeeded Jeroboam II in seeking Assyrian help. Wrong gods lead to wrong policies, so both are appropriate interpretations.

V7: The downfall of the king of Israel is likened to a piece of debris cast away and tossed about on turbulent waters. There seems to be a comparison between the might of the nations and the relative insignificance of Samaria, thus cutting down to size this rebellious little nation. The comparison is heightened by the realisation that it is the Lord who controls the waters. What folly was their disregard of him!

V8: Aven, 'wickedness', is a further reference to the idolatry first instituted at Bethel and spoken of here as 'the sin of Israel'. The shrines displayed the sin of Israel in forsaking God.

Thorn and thistle symbolise God's curse on the idolatrous sanctuaries. They are first mentioned as symbolic of the curse of God on the disobedience of Adam and Eve (*Gen.* 3:18).

They shall say to the mountains. These words, later quoted by Jesus on his way to the cross (*Luke* 23:30), express the fear and terror of those who have rejected him. Also connected with the final judgement of God (*Rev.* 6:16), they express the hope-lessness of those who realise the terror of the judgement and the impossibility of escape. We are reminded of the awesome reality of the divine judgement. In wrath, God remembers mercy, but his love does not discard the claims of his holy law.

This highlights the significance of the truth that Jesus 'was made to be sin for us'. The mountains and hills cannot cover the guilt of the sinner, but the blood of Jesus can! How shall we escape if we neglect so great a salvation (*Heb.* 2:1–3; 10:31)?

V9: Again the prophet refers to what happened at Gibeah (*Hos.* 9:9, *Judg.* 19–20). The judgement here sounds awful, but the nation was being reminded of how richly it deserved its fate. They had sinned dreadfully and persistently. Calvin comments: 'The nation did indeed avenge the deed at Gibeah on the men of Benjamin, but they are wholly like them. Jehu had likewise been an instrument of chastening, yet God calls him a murderer.'

There they stood (NIV: 'have remained'). They had persisted in their sin.

The battle in Gibeah. This part of the verse is variously understood. The NKJ seems to suggest that the full punishment due to Gibeah did not take place. Another possibility is that the war in Gibeah was because of 'the sons of wickedness', the wicked men of Benjamin. The NIV has: 'Did not war overtake the evildoers in Gibeah?'

It is suggested that the sin at Gibeah had never been adequately called to account, but that account would now be rendered on the nation as a whole. The sin at Gibeah was a particular matter, but because it had become part of the habit of the nation's life it would inevitably be called to account.

The patience of God is seen here in that centuries had passed during which God had not fully called this sin to account. But the righteousness of God is also seen in that the sin would not be passed by. The wilfulness of Israel is seen in that the pattern of sin had been continued through the generations, even though they had been instruments in its punishment at the time. They had learned nothing from the forbearance of God.

V10: God's absolute sovereignty is emphasised. God would punish them in his time, and the nations would be his instrument. When the disasters began to come upon Israel, it was not because God was unable to protect them, but because he was sovereignly using the nations to bring judgement upon them for their persistent rebellion. Their alliances with those nations would not save them from God's use of these very nations to express his wrath.

Their two transgressions (NIV: 'double sin'). Various attempts have been made to explain this:

The idols at Bethel and Dan;

The double sin of apostasy from God and rebellion from the house of David;

That the nations would bind Israel and Judah as Samson was bound and made to serve;

Most simply, in the sense of the 'full measure' of punishment (*Isa.* 40:2), or of Joseph's 'double portion' as the favoured son.

Calvin suggests that however much they bound themselves together to gain strength, it would be easy for God to bring the nations together to punish them.

FOR MEDITATION

1. Outline for the chapter:
   a) The *curse of godless Israel*, richly blessed, increasingly wayward.
   b) The *chastisement of the holy God*, inescapable and terrible.
   c) The *call of covenant grace*, although the end seemed imminent (v12).
   d) The *consequence of wilful choice*, complete destruction (v15).

2. V1: The symbol of *the vine* turns our thoughts to Jesus' speaking of himself as the true vine and believers as the branches (*John* 15:1–5). In Hosea, Israel is being rebuked for spiritual fruitlessness; the teaching of Jesus, too, solemnly emphasises the importance of bearing fruit and the awful destiny of fruitless branches (v6).

The Apostle Paul also speaks of our intimate relationship with the Lord Jesus Christ (*Rom.* 6). We have been united with him in his death. This means:

a) that we acknowledge that we are sinners who deserve eternal death, but that he died on our behalf and in our place. The divine wrath against us was turned aside (*Rom.* 3:24–26) as he took upon his sinless soul our guilt before God (*Gal.* 3:13).

b) that we 'die to sin' – we renounce it. Because he has ransomed us we have been delivered from its lordship. We turn our backs on its promised delights and indulgences.

c) that we have also been united with him in his resurrection. Clothed with his perfect righteousness, we have new power and inclination to live in a new way. We have been handed over to the rule of righteousness (*Rom.* 6:16–18), to live in the power of the Holy Spirit (*Rom.* 8:2).

What is the fruit we are now expected to bear? Remember Jesus said, 'By their fruits you will know them', and Paul speaks of 'being fruitful in every good work' (*Col.* 1:10; see also *Luke* 3:8, *John* 15:7–12, *Rom.* 6:22, *Gal.* 5:22–23, *Eph.* 5:9, *Heb.* 12:11, *James* 3:17–18).

3. V1: The *luxuriant* or *empty vine*. This teaches the same principle as Jesus' lesson on the barren fig tree which he cursed on his way into Jerusalem (*Mark* 11:12–14; 20–21). Both depict the empty professions and outward forms of religion of Israel, barren of the spiritual fruit required by God. Hosea was teaching that the fruit of all the divine blessings on Israel was being selfishly consumed. Our Lord took hold of the same idea in the parable of the wicked vine-dressers (*Matt.* 21:33–41), whose scheme was to seize the master's vineyard for themselves.

We must ask ourselves whether the many blessings God has showered upon us are also being selfishly consumed. When we receive an increase in wages, does Christian work benefit? Do the poor and deprived benefit? Or does it merely mean more luxury at home? Do we build our beautiful houses while the Lord's house lies waste (*Hag.* 1:4)? Maybe we are like the Jews in Haggai's day, earning wages '*to put* into a bag with holes' – wealthy but unsatisfied.

John Wesley and Hudson Taylor are both known to have continued to live on their previous salary when their pay increased, so that they might give more to the Lord's work. The following extract from Hudson Taylor's diary shows the deep sense of commitment of that outstanding missionary leader.

Having now the twofold object in view of accustoming myself to endure hardness and of economising in order to help those among whom I was labouring in the gospel, I soon found out that I could live upon very much less than I had previously thought possible. I found that by living mainly upon oatmeal and rice, with occasional variations, a very small sum was sufficient for my needs. In this way I had more than two thirds of my income available for other purposes, and my experience was that the less I spent on myself and the more I gave to others, the fuller of happiness and blessing did my soul become.[1]

We have much to learn about fruitfulness!

4. V2: *The divided heart.* We should ask the Lord regularly to show us whether our heart is divided (*Psa.* 139:23–24). He reminds us that where our heart is, there will our treasure be (*Matt.* 6:21). We may be able to deceive ourselves, but the Lord knows our heart. The word translated 'divided' can mean 'smooth', and we can become smooth, adept at mouthing evangelical truths and doing the right things, but without real love for Christ. Like a tyre with a badly worn tread, we can go through the motions without any real grip; that is dangerous, whether on the motorway or on the highway of life. Preaching on this subject, C.H. Spurgeon noted the following as the usual symptoms of the divided heart:[2]

a) Formality in worship. 'People who know nothing of the power of the gospel contend for these little shells because they have nothing of the kernel.'

b) Inconsistency. 'You appear to run first of all with God's people and then afterwards with the multitude to do evil.'

c) Variability in object. 'They are sometimes hot and feverish and anon, they are chilly and cold.'

d) Frivolity in religion. 'When we can quote texts of scripture to make jest of them, when we can come to the Lord's table as though it were a common repast, then I fear our heart is divided. I know that any soul conscious of its guilt, if it has really been brought to know the love of Christ, will always come to sacred things in a sacred manner.'

[1] Hudson Taylor, *Retrospect* (London: OMF Books, 1974), p.20.
[2] From 'A Divided Heart', No 276, in *The New Park Street Pulpit, Containing Sermons of the Rev C H Spurgeon, Vol. V* (London: Passmore & Alabaster, 1860), pp.409–416.

Spurgeon further notes the sad effects of a divided heart:

a) A divided heart is a sad heart. The bird that seeks to find rest upon two twigs can never have peace; and the soul that endeavours to find two resting places, first in the world and then in the Saviour, will never have joy or comfort. Hence David says, 'Unite my heart to fear Your name' (*Psa.* 86:11).

b) A divided heart is useless in the church. 'We cannot put him into the pulpit to propound a gospel he does not practise. We cannot put him into a deaconship to serve the church, which his life would ruin. In no respect is he any good to us. His name may be on the church books, but it had better be taken away.'

c) A divided heart is dangerous in the world. 'Such a man is like a leper going abroad in the midst of healthy people; he spreads the disease. He says he is a Christian and is admitted into all society, and yet inwardly he is full of all rottenness and deception.'

d) Finally such a man is reprobate in the sight of God. 'If there is a place where sinners are more loathsome to God than any other, it is in his church. A dog in his kennel is well enough, but a dog in the throne room is quite out of place.'

On the matter of the loathsomeness of the divided heart, Spurgeon notes that it is chronic and difficult to cure because it is a flattering disease. 'The text might be rendered "their heart flatters them, now they are found faulty". There are many cunning flatterers in the world, but the most cunning is a man's own heart. A man's own heart will flatter him even about his sins: the heart turns bitter into sweet and sweet into bitter. It is so deceitful above all things and desperately wicked that it has the wickedness to put darkness for light and light for darkness.'

> *Is there a thing beneath the sun*
> *That strives with thee my heart to share,*
> *Ah, tear it thence, and reign alone,*
> *The Lord of every motion there.*
>
> – Gerhard Tersteegen

5. V3: *We have no king.* The Jews of a later day boasted that they had no king but Caesar, and in many respects they may be likened to the Jews of Hosea's time. Both had cast off their allegiance to the Lord and had in fact sold themselves into bondage. A nation seeking to throw off the rule of God will find itself enslaved by men. God is the king! The Jews of Jesus' day boasted that they were never in bondage to any man, but in that boast they were deceived. In fact they were in double bondage. Politically they were in the iron grip of Rome, though they were allowed some measure of self rule; religiously they were in even more rigorous bondage to the man-made system of the Pharisees.

Anyone who seeks to throw off the rule of God will find himself under some other yoke, whether a political system, an enslaving ideology, a false religion or just self! The word from which we derive 'despot' is applied in the Scriptures to the Lord Jesus Christ. It means 'an absolute ruler'. Paul delighted to call himself 'the bondslave of Jesus Christ'. When we repent, we receive him as the absolute ruler of our life. The centurion who came to Jesus to heal his servant recognised that it was the man who was under authority who had authority. The same principle applies to those under the authority of God: they experience the delivering power of God, whose service is 'perfect freedom' (*John* 8:36).

Chapter 10:11–15

Urgent Appeal and Solemn Warning

V11: **A trained heifer.** Israel is likened to a well-trained and healthy animal. The verse speaks of God's grace and tender care for his people from the early days when the nation could not help itself. The nation is compared to a heifer, which enjoyed the easy work of threshing and the opportunity to eat her fill (*Deut.* 25:4). This would be a fair picture of Israel during the long and prosperous reign of Jeroboam II.

Some have thought it referred to Israel's delight in treading others down, but since Jeroboam did not have a great reputation as a conqueror and military oppressor, this is not likely.

But I harnessed her fair neck (NIV and NASB treat this as future). The prophecy will surely be fulfilled.

I will make Ephraim pull *a plow*. The Lord had previously dealt with the nation with great gentleness and compassion but would now adopt sterner measures. The heifer would now have a rider to drive her and would be made to do the heavy work of ploughing.

The fair neck, which had known no heavy yoke, would now be made to bear one. Matthew Henry interprets: 'I will tame them and make them to be ridden by the Assyrian and other conquerors.' He quotes the comment of a Dr Pocock that 'God has dealt with them as a husbandman does with the cattle he trains for service. He took hold of her fair neck and harnessed her with the yoke of his commandments, that being trained in his institutions she might not be tempted with the usages of the heathen. He employed all fair and likely means to keep them in obedience with precepts proper to them, yet they turned aside.'

Judah shall plow. Although not yet so far into apostasy as Israel, Judah is also warned. The Lord was aware of the spiritual state of Judah, although this was not so apparent to men. In the reign of Ahaz and again in the reign of Hezekiah, Judah suffered from invasions which, in fact, were the beginning of the end for the kingdom.

Jacob may well refer to the whole nation. Both parts of the nation were under threat, since the Lord could read the hearts of all. Judah under Hezekiah was at the time experiencing something of a spiritual revival, but it did not really touch the heart of the nation.

Break his clods. Breaking the clods was the hardest kind of ploughing, indicating the Lord's severe dealing with them.

V12: Even as God threatened the ploughing of judgement, he offered mercy by calling for 'the ploughing of repentance'. Repentance does not merit forgiveness but is the divinely appointed means of restoration. It is the gift of God (*2 Tim.* 2:15) and expresses a change of heart.

Sow for yourselves righteousness may speak of the practical fruit of righteousness, which is the evidence of true repentance (*Luke* 3:8–14); or perhaps of the exercise of faith which God counted as righteousness for Abraham (*Gen.* 15:6). In Scripture, the way of salvation is always dependent on the righteousness provided by God and received by faith alone. Hosea had made very clear that at this time they were 'sowing to the flesh' (ch 7). If they were to escape they must change their attitude and behaviour.

Reap in mercy. Poole comments that this may apply to human behaviour as well as to the activity of God. True repentance includes both righteousness and mercy. A right attitude to God and mercy in relation to fellow human beings are both required and must be learned through the operation of the Spirit of God. Those who would but turn to God and express repentance in their actions would find him rich in mercy.

Break up your fallow ground. The human heart is likened to a fallow field overgrown with weeds and thorns, untouched by order or by the beauty and fruitfulness of cultivation. The human heart untouched by divine grace is insensitive to its sin. It is overrun by all kinds of self-indulgence and barren of the spiritual fruit God requires of men.

It is **time to seek the LORD.** Hosea here issues an urgent call. It is a miracle of grace that after so much sin and impenitence, and in spite of the solemn threat of judgement, there was still opportunity to turn to the Lord. The storm clouds were gathering; the need for mercy was urgent. If the nation was to be saved at all, it must seek the Lord. The prophets state absolutely that God is sovereign. Yet also, as here, they emphasise the responsibility of man.

Till He comes. This signifies both submission and confidence. It is acknowledged that he will come 'in his time', but he will come. They were assured of that.

Rain righteousness (cf. *Psa.* 72:6–7). God's dealings are abundant in mercy. If they will turn to him, he will pour out the rewards of righteousness. One is tempted to suggest that the 'justifying righteousness' of God may again be in view here.

V13: The promise is followed by a repetition of God's assessment of their present behaviour. NKJ continues the 'ploughing' imagery; NIV has 'planted'. Both convey a telling comparison: in relation to God they had loved the easy task (v11), but in relation to sin, they were willing to put forth effort. They had shown great industry in the cause of sin.

You have reaped iniquity. As with verse 12, this may refer either to the activity of man or to the judgement which God would bring upon them for their sin. So it may mean, either 'you have persisted in your evil ways', or 'you have begun to feel the consequences of your evil course'.

You have eaten the fruit of lies. They had fed themselves on vain hopes, trusting the lies of their false prophets and their idols.

You trusted in your own way. Here was the root of the trouble. All other sins stemmed from their turning to their own way (*Isa.* 53:6).

The multitude of your mighty men. Trust in self, as opposed to trust in God, leads to materialism and militarism. Both are vain hopes (*Jer.* 17:5–7).

The principle expounded in this section is 'sowing and reaping'. They were being encouraged to sow 'to the Lord' and to reap the abundant blessing of righteousness and mercy. Instead they were following their own deeply entrenched instincts for sin and rebellion, and they would reap destruction.

V14: **Tumult** (NIV: 'the roar of battle'). They would experience devastation by invading armies, and all their fortresses would be overthrown.

Shalman may refer to an invasion by Shalmaneser I in the days of Jehu, or possibly to Salmanu, a Moabite king who was tributary to Tiglath Pileser of Assyria. Nothing is known of the incident recorded here, but it appears to have been a by-word for severity.

V15: **Bethel** is referred to as typical of the idolatry and godless-ness of the Northern Kingdom.

At dawn may indicate the sudden nature of the overthrow; or possibly 'at a time when better things were hoped for'; or even 'as sure as the day dawns'.

The king of Israel. The intention is doubtless to include the whole nation, although the last king of Israel, Hoshea, may be

[157]

particularly in view as the one who encouraged them in their folly.

FOR MEDITATION

1. Outline for 10:11–15.
   a) *Recognising the time.* The Lord may still be sought when facing the threat of judgement.
   b) *Returning to the Lord.* Repentance requires a change of behaviour, expressing commitment to him.
   c) *Rejoicing in the promise.* He promises good to those who seek him with all their heart.
   d) *Receiving the consequences of sin.* Where there is no repentance there will be disaster.

2. Vv11–12: Before God judges, he gives ample and clear warning to repent. His method is twofold; first, in his Word given through the prophets, and second, in his providential chastening (when things go wrong!). He promises that we shall hear a word behind us (*Isa.* 30:21). We need to keep our spiritual senses tuned to respond to the slightest whispers of his correction. We should learn to make Psalm 139:23–24 our daily prayer, that God may search us, keep us from folly and lead us in the way everlasting. The prayer of Psalm 119:36–37 is also appropriate.

3. Contrast the 'yoke' implied in verse 11 with that spoken of by Jesus (*Matt.* 11:30). Which yoke we bear depends on what we do with the Lord Jesus Christ and his invitation to come to him. He promises a light yoke and an easy burden. The Jews in the time of Hosea were rejecting the ministry of God's grace; hence, their burden was heavy. The yoke of discipline is necessary that we may grow spiritually, as is seen even in the life of Jesus (*Heb.* 5:8). But Hosea is speaking here of a yoke of judgement caused by sin.

4. V12: *Sow righteousness.* Sowing is a continuous process, and the life of the Christian should be one of continuous action. We are to be diligent in making our calling and election sure (*2 Pet.* 1:10). Righteousness, defined by Matthew Henry as 'doing our duty in dependence upon the grace of God', is to be the wellspring of our activity. This righteousness entails a right attitude of dependence and obedience towards God, an adequate knowledge and acceptance of his law, and mercy in our dealings with others as God has shown mercy to us (*Matt.* 6:12, *Eph.* 4:32–5:3, *Col.* 3:12–13).

5. V12: *Reap in mercy.* The phrase may refer to God's dealings with us. When we seek to walk in his righteousness we may be sure of his mercy (*Psa.* 16:8). 'We reap not in merit, but in mercy' (Matthew Henry).

The phrase may equally apply to our dealings with others, as we learn from God to accept in mercy what they are and what they do to us. We do not look for faults and react in carping criticism, but instead try to express the down-stooping compassion of the Lord Jesus Christ (*Phil.* 2:1–5).

6. V12: *Break up the fallow ground.* We must learn to accept God's verdict on the empty and wilderness places in our life, to be willing to correct wrongs and re-deploy what is being used undesirably or in self-indulgence. Matthew Henry comments: 'Let them cleanse their hearts from all corrupt affections and lusts, which are as weeds or thorns, and let them be humbled for their sins and be of a broken and contrite spirit in the sense of them. Let them be full of sorrow and shame at the remembrance of them, and prepare to receive the divine precepts as the ground is ploughed to receive the seed.'

Look at Psalm 51:17, Jeremiah 31:33; 32:39–40, and Ezekiel 36:31. These show: a) a humbled heart ready to seek the Lord and acknowledge full dependence upon him; b) a hatred of sin, the seeking of righteousness and admitting need for mercy; and c) a holy allegiance and anticipation of the Lord's coming to rain righteousness upon his people.

7. V12: *Seeking God.* Read Isaiah 55:6–7 and Haggai 1. The following are vital principles:

a) Acknowledge the urgency of the situation (*Amos* 4:12, *Isa.* 55:6).

b) Appreciate the mercy of God in offering a way of escape (*Mic.* 7:7–8).

c) Accept the price of discipleship (*Mark* 8:34).

d) Appropriate the abundance of God's grace (*Psa.* 36:5–9, *John* 10:10).

Repentance is man's responsibility, yet it is purely the gift of God. To the elect of God, his commands are his enablings. Obedience is the evidence of the presence of grace.

8. V12: When the Lord comes, *he rains righteousness.* In the dealings of grace there is always an abundance (*Isa.* 44:3; 58:11, *Ezek.* 34:26, *John* 7:37–39;10:10, *Eph.* 3:20). We must ask ourselves whether we are enjoying this abundance and continue to seek it earnestly. We can be too easily satisfied with what the hymn writer calls 'mercy drops', when the Lord desires to send showers of blessing, but he requires that we seek this fullness (*Ezek.* 36:37). Notice how the dealings of grace beget righteous living (*Col.* 3:1–3).

9. From verses 1, 2, and 13 we may deduce a sequence:

a) The gracious dealings of the Lord, who pours upon his people the rich fruits of blessing.

b) The grasping heart of man, who snatches at these things for himself.

c) The growth of division in the heart caused by the conflict between our sense of duty owed to grace and the desire for self-determination.

d) The gods who are the fruit of lies and do not deliver what they promise.

e) The grievous weight of the final judgement.

f) The gracious call to repent before it is too late.

10. The balance between human activity and the divine grace is well illustrated in a sermon of Dr Martyn Lloyd-Jones on 2 Peter 1:5–7 in the light of the previous verses of that chapter:

> The first statement of the gospel is not an exhortation to action or to conduct and behaviour. Before a man is called upon to do anything, he must have received something. Before God calls upon a man to put anything into practice, he has made it possible for man to put it into practice. New Testament analogies put this point quite clearly. We can look at it like this. There is no point in addressing an appeal to a dead person. The only person to whom with any logic you can address an appeal is one who is alive; and that is precisely the teaching of the gospel. When a man becomes a Christian, he is 'born again'; whereas he was dead, he now lives. The Bible compares it to a birth. Before there can be activity there must be life, there must be muscles, there must be the faculties and the propensities. And that is the position of the Christian; he has been given all this. He has these muscles, these spiritual muscles – all things pertaining to life and godliness are given. Therefore, because of this, 'add to your faith', etc. Or take the analogy of a farm, which is a very good one. The whole statement of the gospel is that the farm as such is given to us by God's gift: 'by grace are ye saved through faith; and that not of yourselves: it is the gift of God'. We are given the farm, we are given the implements and all that is necessary, we are given the seed. What we are called upon to do, is to farm. It is no use telling a man to farm if he has not a farm; if he is without land and without seed and without implements, nothing can be done. But all this is given to us,

and therefore, having received them, we are asked to farm. But even then we are reminded that that does not guarantee the increase. 'It is God who gives the increase.' The farmer may plough and harrow, he may roll the land and sow the seed, but in the absence of the rain and the sunshine, and many other factors, there will be no increase. Now there, it seems to me, is the perfect balance which is ever preserved in the New Testament.[1]

[1] In *Expository Sermons on 2 Peter* (Edinburgh: Banner of Truth, 1999), pp.23–24.

Chapter 11:1–7

God's Love and Israel's Ingratitude

V1: God's relationship with Israel and his great love for them are likened to the tender affection of a father for his only son. This had been demonstrated in the early days of their nationhood and is summed up in the confession of the Israelites bringing their first fruits to the Lord: 'My father *was* a Syrian about to perish . . . The Egyptians mistreated us . . . We cried out to the LORD . . . The LORD brought us out of Egypt . . . and has given us this land' (*Deut.* 26:5–9).

Out of Egypt I called My son. Here was the outstanding expression of the divine love: he chose to lay his hand on a slave people who had forgotten the high destiny he had promised to their ancestors. He delivered them from the bondage of Egypt and gave them a new inheritance that expressed their status as sons.

The words are applied to the Lord Jesus Christ (*Matt.* 2:15). See Calvin's comment, p.169.

V2: *As* **they called them, so they went from them.** The NIV follows the Greek Septuagint: 'The more I called them the more they went from me.' Some suggest that the first 'they' could refer to the prophets, others that it may refer to the pagan peoples, like the daughters of Moab (*Num.* 25:2). Either way, the truth is that the people persistently followed the course of rebellion in spite of the Lord's patient endeavours to recall them.

They sacrificed to the Baals. They turned from the true God to false gods (*Judg.* 2:11–13), but in so doing, they did not escape from the requirements of religion. Sacrifices continued to be offered and incense burned, but what had been ordained for them as glad expressions of faith in the grace of God became the expressions of bondage to the Baals and their consorts. When people forsake the worship of the true God, they quickly become slaves to other objects of worship which cannot save. It has been well said that when people turn away from God, they do not worship nothing, but anything!

V3: **I taught Ephraim to walk.** God is pictured as a father teaching the child to walk. He had taken Israel as a helpless baby and taught him to walk and the way to go; but for his grace the Israelites would have perished quickly (*Deut.* 26:5). Calvin interprets: 'I led Israel on foot . . . I humbled myself as mothers are wont to do . . . They were treated by God in an indulgent and paternal manner.'

Taking them by their arms. The relationship was gentle and intimate as the infinite almighty God accommodated himself to their weakness and insignificance, an idea particularly associated with Deuteronomy (see *Deut.* 1:31; 32:11, *Num.* 11:12, *Isa.* 63:9).

I healed them. Many times the Lord had saved them from death, as when the serpents attacked them in the wilderness (*Num.* 21:4–9). The primary idea is of God's providing a way of escape from the consequences of their sin. Jesus mentioned this incident in his conversation with Nicodemus (*John* 3). The term 'healing' in Scripture often indicates spiritual renewal.

But they did not know. Perversely, they would not acknowledge that their deliverance was from God.

What happened ultimately in the case of the bronze serpent mentioned above was typical of them: the people began to burn incense to it, worshipping the creature rather than the creator (*2 Kings* 18:4, *Rom.* 1:25). In his reforming zeal, King Hezekiah removed and destroyed it, but he could not remove the spirit of idolatry from the hearts of the people. It is saddening to realise that the signs God himself gave to point men and women to Christ have been debased by the sinfulness of the human heart. Even in our churches, the standards of God's Word and the life-giving energy of the Holy Spirit have often been displaced by various devices of human wisdom and denominational deviations.

V4: **I drew them with gentle cords** (NIV: 'cords of human kindness'; NASB: 'the cords of a man' [literal]). In spite of their perverseness, the Lord had not dealt with them in wrath but had gently drawn them in love. In the second part of the verse, the imagery changes from that of the parent and the child to that of the farmer and his animal, but the lesson is the same. Some have argued that the expression means 'cords suitable to a man', but that fails to do justice to the tenderness of God, who was himself prepared to become man in order to seek and to save that which was lost (*Luke* 19:10). These were cords not of calculated efficiency, but of compassionate concern.

The word 'draw' is a strong one. It is used of drawing Joseph out of the pit (*Gen.* 39:11) and of rescuing Jeremiah out of the dungeon (*Jer.* 38:13). It also expresses the drawing of God's loving kindness (*Jer.* 31:3). Jesus emphasised that the perverseness of the human heart was so great that no one would come to him unless the Father drew him (*John* 6:44). In the cross we have the supreme demonstration of this magnetism of God (*John* 12:32).

At the beginning of Hosea's prophecy a parallel is drawn between the love of God for his people and the relationship of the prophet with his wife. In that parallel we see the awful perverseness of the heart that refuses all gentleness and compassion. Ultimately the prophecy brings us face to face with the all-conquering power of the divine love, perfectly demonstrated in 14:4.

Bands of love. The constraining power of God is the power of his love, drawing sinners to himself (*Rom.* 5:8). Calvin interprets: 'I have not governed them otherwise than a father does his children. I have not laid on them a servile yoke, nor one such as is laid upon a brute beast, but I was content with parental discipline.'

I was to them as those who take the yoke from their neck. This illustrates the thoughtful driver who gives the toiling animal rest, allowing it to eat comfortably. Israel had forged for itself a yoke of bondage, particularly in the reign of Ahab. But in the long reign of Jeroboam II, although they had deserved his judgement and wrath, the Lord had eased the yoke and allowed them to feed on prosperity. This very suitably completes the idea of 'the cords of a man': in spite of all their stubborn sinfulness, God had continued to deal with them in gentleness.

V5: He shall not return to Egypt but Assyria shall be his king. The NIV renders this as a question: 'Shall he not return to Egypt and will not Assyria rule over them?' The NIV follows the idea of 8:13 and 9:3, in which a return to Egypt is mentioned. One explanation is that the return to Egypt would not be literal. The prophet was speaking symbolically, saying that the bondage in Assyria would be equally bitter.

V6: The sword shall slash. In his dealings with them in the past, God had always given them breathing space because his aim had been corrective. But now he is dealing with them in judgement which is penal.

Devour his districts (NIV: 'destroy the bars of their gates'). The Hebrew word is problematical. It is used more than thirty times in the Pentateuch to refer to 'poles' in the furnishings of the tabernacle. It is also translated 'boasters', where 'liars' and 'sorcerers' have also been suggested (*Jer.* 50:36). Calvin translates the word here as 'bolts'. He sees it as a substitution of a part for the whole, indicating a wholesale destruction of their defences. The inference is clear that all the things in which they have trusted will be shown to be impotent.

Because of their own counsels (NIV: 'will put an end to their plans'). They will be destroyed because of their self-will. This may refer to the conspiracy of Hoshea, the last king of Israel, with So, the king of Egypt. Far from helping them, their scheming had brought forward the judgement

When men trust their own wisdom rather than the Lord, they bring upon themselves grief. The burden of Jeremiah to Judah over a century later was very similar (*Jer.* 42:7–18). Calvin comments: 'Since then, they who despise God, seem to themselves to be very wise and to be fortified by their good counsels, the prophet shows that the ruin to the Israelites would be that they were swollen with this diabolical prudence and would not condescend to obey the Word of the Lord.'

Jeremiah warns against such false wisdom (*Jer.* 9:23–24).

V7: My people are bent on backsliding from Me (NIV: 'determined to turn from me'). Laetsch, the Lutheran commentator, suggests 'impaled on their apostasy from me', and one might suggest 'bent on staying bent'.

The Hebrew of the last part of the verse has been variously understood:

a) Even if they called upon God, he would not re-instate them (because of the perverseness of their hearts);

b) Even though the prophets called them back to God, they would not exalt him;

c) Even when they call upon God they do not exalt him;

d) They call upon their 'high god' (a false deity), but he will not be able to lift them up.

Whichever alternative is adopted, the sense is conveyed of the utterly lost state of the nation.

FOR MEDITATION

1. Outline for the whole chapter.
   a) The *way of a wilful nation.* They have continually abused the compassionate grace of God.
   b) *The wages of sin* (vv5–7). They are appointed for the yoke of bondage. How can a Holy God remit such a debt? (*Isa.* 53, *1 Pet.* 2:24).
   c) *The wonder of grace* (vv8–9). God will not give them up, though that is what they deserve.
   d) *The work of restoration* (v10–11). The lion's call and the trembling return.
   e) *The warning to Judah* (v12). A warning against presumption. Think of the command of the Lord Jesus in the garden of Gethsemane, 'Watch and pray' (*Matt.* 26:41). He knows our vulnerability and warns and encourages, so that we are on guard against it.

2. Many aspects of God's grace are gathered up into that one word 'called':

The sovereign love that chose us (*John* 15:16, *Rom.* 9:29–30).

The redeeming grace that laid hold of the slaves of sin (*Isa.* 43:1–2, *1 Pet.* 1:2).

The delivering power that brought sinners out of the house of bondage (*Deut.* 7:8, *Eph.* 2:1–4).

The continuing guidance and provision that brought them safely through the sea and the wilderness (*Exod.* 15:13, *Deut.* 8:3–5, *Phil.* 4:19).

The perfect teaching of the law, like a father's guidance for his children (*Psa.* 32:8).

The triumphant patience that refuses to give them up (*Isa.* 63:9).

The glorious inheritance of the promised land, and the believer's heavenly inheritance (*1 Pet.* 1:3–4).

3. Thomas Brooks on 11:1:

> Where God loves, he loves to the end . . . As Joseph's heart was full of love to his brethren even then when he spoke roughly to them and withdrew himself from them, for he was fain to go aside and ease his heart by weeping; so the heart of God is full of love for his people, even then when he seems to be most displeased with them and to turn his back upon them. Though God's dispensations may seem changeable towards his people, yet his gracious disposition is unchangeable towards them . . . The mother's bowels cannot more yearn after the tender babe, than God doth after his distressed ones.[1]

4. This people had been trading on God's love and gentleness, his goodness and longsuffering; but now at length, the day of reckoning had been called. For those who suggest that the teaching of the New Testament is different, the words of Jesus should be a sufficient answer (*Matt.* 23:37–39). When the redeeming love of the only one who can rescue us has been persistently and wilfully rejected, we are left to ourselves. The end of that road is desolation (*Heb.* 6,10).

5. The phrase '*Out of Egypt I called my son*', is applied to Jesus by Matthew (*Matt.* 2:15). Calvin comments:

> It behoves us to consider this, that God, when he formerly redeemed his people from Egypt, only showed by a certain prelude the redemption which he deferred till the coming of Christ. Hence, as the body was then brought forth from Egypt into Judaea, so at length the head also came forth from Egypt: and then God fully showed him to be the true deliverer of his people. Matthew therefore most fitly accommodates this passage to Christ, that God loved his Son from his first childhood and called him from Egypt. We know at the same time that Christ

---

[1] From 'The Mute Christian under the Smarting Rod', in *Works of Thomas Brooks, Vol.1* (Edinburgh: Banner of Truth, 1980), pp.372–373.

is called the Son of God in a respect different from the people of Israel; for adoption made the children of Abraham the children of God, but Christ is by nature the 'only begotten Son of God'.

The phrase reminds us too of the essential relationship between the Old and New Testaments:

> *The New is in the Old concealed*
> *The Old is by the New revealed.*

6. V3: *I taught Ephraim to walk, holding them by the arms* illustrates the gentleness of the fatherhood of God. When one becomes a Christian, he has been born 'from above'; now he must learn to walk (*Col.* 2:6–7). God enables the new believer to do this as he continues the 'good work' he has begun in regeneration (*John* 1:12–13, *Phil.* 1:6). The New Testament makes much of the analogy of the Christian life as a walk. It teaches that we must walk worthy (*Col.* 1:10; 2:6–7, *Eph.* 4:1); we must walk in love (*Eph.* 5:2); we must walk as children of light (*Eph.* 5:8); and that we must walk as wise, redeeming the time (*Eph.* 5:15).

7. V3: *I healed them.* He is the God who heals. He had revealed himself under that title at Marah (*Exod.* 15:26). In the New Testament the Lord Jesus was pleased to reveal himself as the physician of the sin-sick soul (*Mark* 2:17). The healing miracles were something of a visual aid to his spiritual ministry. The invitation of Matthew 11:28–30 has never been withdrawn; he is still the perfect doctor for the sin-sick soul.

We must go to him, being honest about our symptoms, not covering anything up, and allowing him to probe.

We must acknowledge the wisdom of the one to whom we are committing our case.

We must accept his diagnosis and submit without qualification to the course of treatment he prescribes, even though this requires radical surgery or a diet that goes against our inclinations. Attitudes will have to be changed and our whole lifestyle transformed.

Are we ready for such a relationship? His call is uncompromising: deny self and take up the cross (*Mark* 8:34–36).

8. V4: *I drew them.* This is illustrated very well in a comment from Matthew Henry on Romans 8:14: 'The Christian is led by the Spirit of God, as a scholar in his learning is led by his tutor, as a traveller is led in his journey by his guide, as a soldier in his engagements by his captain, not driven as a beast, but led as a rational creature, "drawn with the cords of a man".'

9. V4: *Bands of love.* All God's dealings with believers are on the basis of his tender redeeming love. God loved us from eternity past and elected us in Christ. He revealed that love in history by making satisfaction for sin at the cross. He makes that love real in our experience through the work of the Holy Spirit in drawing us to Christ (*Jer.* 31:3, *Rom.* 5:6–8).

His dealings are suitable to our human needs. He understands these perfectly, since he took upon himself the form of a servant and was made in human likeness (*Phil.* 2:7).

His dealings will involve discipline. We need 'cords' because of our proneness to wander (*Psa.* 119:176), but the discipline is always the discipline of love (*Heb.* 12:6). It is true that he says 'Take My yoke'; but he adds, 'for My yoke *is* easy and My burden is light.'

10. Vv5–6: *Judgement.* The confusion of sinners is of their own contrivance. God's counsels would have saved them; their own counsels contrived their ruin' (Matthew Henry).

Chapter 11:8–11

God's Pity

Even in wrath, God shows his tender pity. The rebellious people deserved only to be consumed by his wrath, but even now after so many warnings and acts of discipline, he would restrain his wrath for his mercy's sake (*Psa.* 130:3–4).

God is speaking here in human terms, expressing his sovereign purposes in terms comprehensible to them, so that they might see their sinfulness and the awful judgement it deserved and understand the magnitude and miracle of the divine mercy.

V8: Even as he decreed judgement, the Lord remembered his choice of Israel and promised that he would not make a full end of them as he had **Admah** and **Zeboiim**, two wicked cities destroyed like Sodom and Gomorrah (*Deut.* 29:23). Some have noted that Israel is not compared even to Sodom and Gomorrah but to two lesser cities, and suggest that this was deliberate, to humble their pride.

My heart churns within Me. Justice and mercy are in tension (see *Deut.* 32:36). The Lord's justice requires that Israel be punished, but his covenant mercy counters that they should be relieved, a problem which is resolved only at the cross (*Rom.* 3:23–26).

Calvin comments: 'The design is to show that if he dealt with the people of Israel as they deserved, they would now be made like Sodom and Gomorrah. But as God was merciful and embraced his people with paternal affection, he . . . would be willing to grant pardon; as in the case of a father who, on seeing his son's wicked disposition suddenly feels a strong displeasure, and then, being seized with relentings, is inclined to spare him.'

V9: The sovereign nature of the divine mercy is seen: God had commanded the complete overthrow of Admah and Zeboiim, and Israel now deserved the same fate. But God was promising that he would not execute the fierceness of his great anger against them.

I *am* God and not man. Angry men are intent only upon vengeance; but God has higher purposes of grace, to accomplish reconciliation. Some expositors suggest that this mode of expression encourages the faithful to have confidence to hold fast God's promise, even when the wrath breaks out and appears to be all consuming (cf. *Num.* 23:19, *1 Sam.* 15:29, *Isa.* 50:10).

The Holy One in your midst. The people were reminded of two vital consequences of having 'the Holy One' among them. First, they must remember the requirements of his law, that the camp should be without any defilement (*Deut.* 23:14). The failure to observe this was the reason for his anger against them at this time. Second, though his holiness is often the ground for his discipline, on this occasion it is the ground for his exceeding great mercy. He had made a covenant with them and though he would chastise them with the rod of men, he would not take away his mercy (*2 Sam.* 7:14). He had made his promise to be in their midst, and though he would withdraw for a while, he would not entirely forsake.

This may obliquely refer to the sin of Israel with the golden calf (*Exod.* 33–34). After the sin, Moses took the tent of meeting outside the camp and pleaded with the Lord for a revelation of his presence, and the covenant was renewed. The divine displeasure was dramatically demonstrated, but God did not destroy his people.

I will not come with terror (NIV: 'in wrath'). The translation offered by the NKJ and the NIV requires only the emendation of a single vowel point. The Hebrew text, which was followed by the AV, would translate: 'I will not enter into a city', a reading favoured by both Matthew Henry and Calvin. They explain it to mean that God would not enter the city to destroy it as he had destroyed Admah and Zeboiim.

V10: Their attitude would be transformed; their hearts would be inclined to obedience. Surely the teaching of the new covenant is anticipated here (cf. *Jer.* 32:38–40)?

It also suggests that they would be free to follow the Lord, as Calvin points out: 'Many indeed will be the enemies, and many will labour to set up opposition: but the people shall nevertheless come forth free . . . For the Lord will fill all with dread and restrain all the efforts of their enemies.' However, Calvin is of the opinion that the main point here is to show the Lord as the leader of his people. 'As long as the people were scattered in Assyria and in other distant lands, they were without a head, as a mutilated body. But when the ripened time of restoration came, the Lord resolved to deliver them and proclaimed himself the leader of his people; and in this manner the people were gathered to God.'

He will roar like a lion. In Amos the roaring of the lion symbolised the Lord's message of judgement (*Amos* 1:2; 3:8). Here the lion is roaring to call its young. The roar at once inspires terror in all enemies, but to the young it is a token of love and protection. We may think of the roar of the Lion of the Tribe of Judah gathering his scattered people (*Rev.* 5:5).

From the west probably symbolises the gathering from among the Gentile nations (*Isa.* 11:10–12).

V11: **They shall come trembling like a bird.** The imagery is that of the return of a migratory bird and may indicate eagerness rather than fear. The Syriac version combines the ideas of haste and trembling. They would come back from Egypt and Assyria, these powers representing a bondage that seemed inescapable.

As a dove. A common bird in Palestine, the dove was proverbial for swiftness and timidity and reputed to fly faster when frightened. Calvin applies the whole of this description to the Egyptians and Assyrians, saying that when the Lord decreed the return of his people, nothing in the world would nullify it. The Egyptians and Assyrians would be struck with such dread that they would not stir when the Lord restored his people. While Calvin's interpretation expounds a valuable truth concerning the certain triumph of the sovereign love and purposes of God, a reference to Israel is probably more in accordance with the context.

I will let them dwell in their houses. The prophet makes clear that this is the sovereign work of God. This pictures a complete and secure restoration (cf. *Ezek.* 36:33–38). A question arises as to the manner of fulfilment of the prophecy, to which there are at least three possible responses:

a) All prophecies have a condition of repentance, and were forfeited due to Israel's persistent obtuseness. But if the sovereign God's declared intention is to restore, can this be made conditional?

b) This will be fulfilled in the fullness of time in a great restoration of Israel to its own land. Many greatly respected evangelical commentators have held to this view, which has given inspiration for evangelising the Jews. The difficulty is that there is no way today of identifying the tribes of the Northern Kingdom. This may be countered with the assertion that what is impossible with men is possible with God, which cannot be challenged.

c) The prophecy had its fulfilment in part in the time of Ezra, but awaits a more complete spiritual fulfilment in the 'spiritual Israel', the church, in which Jew and Gentile are one

(*Eph.* 2:13–18). Matthew Henry quotes the ancient Jews as assigning the meaning of this passage to the times of Messiah. He refers to Dr Pocock, who sees a prophecy of Christ's coming to preach the gospel to the dispersed children of Israel, the children of God that were scattered abroad (*1 Pet.* 1:1). James appears to use Amos 9:11–12 in this spiritual sense (*Acts* 15:16–17).

FOR MEDITATION

1. V9: *I will not destroy Ephraim.* The ground and reason for this promise is that *I am God.* This encourages us to hope in the divine mercy.

First, we remember God's character. He is Lord over his anger, whereas the anger of men often lords it over them! Human passions are not to be compared with the tender mercies of God, which do not fail and are new every morning (*Lam.* 3:22–23). An earthly prince in such a strait between love and justice would be at a loss. But he who is God can secure both the honour of his justice and his love (*Rom.* 3:24–26).

We also remember what God is to his people. He is the Holy One in their midst, who has bound himself to them by a gracious covenant and will not break his word. In the new covenant, he has promised to redeem and present perfect all those whom he has chosen in Christ (*Rom.* 8:29–30). They will appear spotless before his presence with exceeding joy (*Jude* 24). This should be the incentive to holy living now (*1 John* 3:1–3).

2. V10: *The Lord roars.* The same imagery is used in terms of judgement in Amos 3:4, 8. But here the intention is different, indicating not only discipline but also the voice of encouragement and protection to the young cubs. The Word of the Lord, which threatens judgement upon all ungodliness, is the Word of which the believer says, 'Oh, how I love Your law' (*Psa.* 119:97). This is one of the tests by which we may know that we are truly

his (*John* 14:15, 21, 23; *1 John* 5:3). Assurance of salvation does not lead to presumption in the true believer, because it is guarded by clear teaching about the walk with God which evidences true faith (*2 Tim.* 2:19, *1 John* 2:6, *2 Pet.* 1:5–10). To return to Hosea's analogy, the young cubs hear the parent's roar; they tremble, and walk humbly at the parent's heels.

3. Vv 10–11: How wonderfully the sovereignty of grace and the human response are mirrored here! The longing of the heart of man for God is likened to the homing instinct of the migratory bird. It is the Lord who establishes the believer and makes us secure in Christ, so that it may truly be said that they will run in the way of his commandments when he enlarges the heart (*Psa.* 119:32).

4. Walking after the Lord means: to acknowledge dependence, as we seek him; to adhere to God's standards, as we show mercy; and to accept his guidance, as we seek righteousness.

5. V11: *I will let them dwell in their houses.* The Lord has gone to prepare a place for us and will bring us safely to the place he has prepared. Meanwhile, as we live in obedience, we may know the homely security of his presence (*John* 14:2–3, 23).

Chapter 11:12–12:14

Ephraim Condemned, Judah Warned

Hosea's long ministry was mainly to the Northern Kingdom, but this chapter brings solemn warning to Judah also. Although the two kingdoms had been separated for almost two hundred years, they were still essentially one people and their destinies inseparably intertwined. Each at its own pace and according to its own individual sins took its own course to destruction, but Hosea often hints at the link between them (4:15; 5:10,13; 6:4, 11; 8:14; 10:11). Here the oracle initially addressing Ephraim deals in fact with both parts of the nation.

Most commentators acknowledge that the last verse of chapter 11 belongs to the train of thought of chapter 12. The theme is the identity of the nation in its rebellion, demonstrated by their long and persistent history of backsliding.

V12: **Ephraim has encircled Me with lies.** Jacob, their ancestor, was by nature a deceiver, a 'supplanter'. Ephraim, the Northern Kingdom, had shown itself heir to this unhappy trait.

Commentators have approached the last part of the verse in various ways:

a) **Judah still walks with God** (NKJ). Both Poole and Calvin remark on the comparative faithfulness of Judah. Those who follow this reading have pointed to a contrast between Ephraim, the cheat and liar, the 'Jacob' of the first part of the verse, and Judah, who is still 'Israel', a prince with God.

b) **Judah is unruly with God** (NIV, NASB). Theodore

Laetsch, a Lutheran commentator, points out that the word rendered 'unruly' is found also in Jeremiah 2:21, where it is taken to mean 'to roam' or 'to do as one pleases'. Judah had already been warned by Hosea (5:12–14), and the 'charge' mentioned in 12:2 supports this reading.

Chapter 12

V1: **Ephraim feeds on the wind**. Ephraim was still being encouraged by the words of the false prophets, described by one old writer as 'dreams which prove to be noxious blasts'. They were taking in what they wanted to hear rather than what had real substance. It seems that human nature has changed little!

The east wind was hot, blasting and destructive, as is illustrated by the rapid withering of Jonah's gourd (*Jon.* 4:8).

He daily increases lies. This typifies the religious and social failure of the nation. In religion, they were hypocrites who listened to the lies of the false prophets and false gods. Socially, they swindled and mistrusted one another, being generally bent on deceit.

Desolation (NKJ) was the inevitable consequence of their false ways, since sin is always ultimately destructive. **Violence** (NIV) may be the better translation here; lying and violence seem to have been the twin social sins of Israel, covetousness being the primary source of both.

Assyria; Egypt. The reference to both these powers reflects the frantic and inconsistent attempts of Ephraim to buy their friendship. Palestine was famous for its **oils**, and these were used in the attempt to purchase favours.

V2: **A charge against Judah** may be a reference to the unfortunate tendencies shown at the end of the reign of Uzziah (*2 Chron.* 26:16) or possibly to the blatant apostasy of the reign of Ahaz. Hosea's prophecies are not dated, and it seems that his ministry extended over a very long period.

Jacob may well refer to the ten tribes of the Northern Kingdom, whose punishment will be according to their deserving. Some might consider the Lord's dealing with Israel heavy handed, but the punishment was fully merited. The whole prophecy shows the depth of God's love for his wayward people.

V3: **He took his brother by the heel** (*Gen.* 25:22–26). Calvin observes that Jacob's blessedness was not by his conscious effort but 'by the determined purpose and will of God' (*Gen.* 25:23; *Mal.* 1:2–3; *Rom.* 9:12–13), which should have stirred the nation to gratitude. Some see here the earnestness of Jacob as he sought for the birthright, in contrast with the degeneracy of his descendants. He had sought for the privileges of the firstborn, but they seemed intent on casting them off.

In his strength he struggled with God. Jacob had prevailed by wrestling (*Gen.* 32:24–32), but these people, by contrast, had turned to idols. Jacob at birth had wrestled with his brother, and in his maturity he wrestled with God; but he valued the inheritance promised by God, for which Hosea's generation was showing no respect. This passage may imply that Jacob's self-willed efforts brought him nothing and that only when his strength was broken and he wept did he prevail. The nation to which Hosea was prophesying was also going about it the wrong way – and, we should note, so do we on many occasions!

V4: **He struggled with the Angel and prevailed**. The power that prevailed was that of a helpless man who could only cling to God. One old commentator comments, 'Thus God teaches the irresistible might of conscious weakness', and Israel would have to learn that truth the hard way.

The **angel** referred to here is the 'covenant angel', the pre-incarnate Christ, appearing in the form of a man. The grace of our God, who stoops down to men, was demonstrated in his willingness to wrestle with his servant.

[180]

Matthew Henry comments that Jacob prevailed over his fear, in his prayer for deliverance from Esau, and for the blessing. He prevailed by 'tears and seeking favour'. Israel in Hosea's day had not learned that lesson.

He found Him *in* Bethel. Jacob first came to a personal knowledge of the divine grace at Bethel (*Gen.* 28:11–19), where it was the Lord who found Jacob, not vice versa. This later became the place of rededication (*Gen.* 35:1–15), which again was the result of divine initiative. What a contrast to Hosea's day, when Bethel had become a centre of idolatry! God had found Jacob at this place, but now at this very same place Israel was seeking to cast him off.

There He spoke to us (NIV: 'talked with him'). The plural faithfully reproduces the Hebrew. The people were being reminded that they were the heirs of these rich promises of grace. What God had said to Jacob, he was saying to them now. The love of God and his covenant promises do not change; covenant faithfulness is an essential characteristic of his being.

V5: **The LORD God of hosts.** He is the 'I AM', the God of covenant grace who chose Israel. He is the creator and upholder of the universe, the source of all power, the God of hosts, including the powers of heaven now foolishly worshipped by Israel. They were calling on the sun, moon and stars, yet he was the one who held all these in their place.

His memorable name expresses his being and character. It is 'I AM', represented in our translations as 'Jehovah' or 'Yahweh', and often appearing in capitals as 'the LORD'. In this character he is to be remembered, and here his abiding faithfulness is reiterated. In the realm of nature, his faithfulness upholds the universe from day to day. The same faithfulness is found in his grace in the covenant, as redeemer and sustainer of his people.

V6: The very remembrance of the Name plainly spells out a call to repentance. Their hope for the future was in returning to him. They must walk before him in obedience and submission, practising mercy and justice (6:1–3;10:12). This is what it is to 'wait' on him (*Psa.* 130).

V7: **A cunning Canaanite** (NIV: 'merchant'). This is a play on words, since the word means both 'Canaanite' and 'merchant'. These sons of Jacob had become like the Canaanites they had been commanded to exterminate. This was the greatest reproach that could be heaped upon them.

Deceitful scales. The law of Moses indicted dishonest weights and measures (*Lev.* 19:36; *Deut.* 25:13, 15). The expression here applies to commercial deceit and fraud of every kind. Calvin says: 'The deceitful balance may be extended to all their dissimulations, fallacies and falsehoods by which God, as he had before complained, was surrounded.'

Oppress (NIV: 'defraud'). The word may denote both open violence and the oppression of the poor. It is used a number of times by the prophets to describe the rich oppressing the poor; it also describes the Assyrian treatment of Israel (*Isa.* 52:4).

V8: In spite of God's indictment, they were glorying in their temporary prosperity, reckoning it as an indication of divine favour or of the emptiness of the prophet's threats.

The Hebrew of the last part of the verse is difficult, but the sense is that they gloried in their skill and success and imagined that they would never be called to account as guilty sinners. Theirs was a society in which wealth and business success meant everything, and there was no thought of guilt. This part of the prophecy may date from the reign of Jeroboam II, when the kingdom was enjoying a period of wealth. If it comes from a later period, it demonstrates how utterly blind they had become, unable to see the danger signs.

V9: The Lord's reply to Ephraim's false boasts of security was that in spite of everything, they were still God's people. Had he not redeemed them from Egypt? They were still in his hand; he was their covenant God.

I will again make you dwell in tents. Some commentators see this as a threat that all their wealthy pomp would be stripped away and they would again be reduced to dwelling in tents but, in the light of what follows, most see it as a promise of a national renewal.

As in the days of the appointed feasts. This is generally taken to imply that they would again celebrate the Feast of Tabernacles as commemorative of a mighty deliverance of God. Leon Wood sees a reference to the captivity, but with the implication that even in this God would provide for them. The sovereign power of Jehovah is clearly emphasised. They will be disciplined as in the former days of the wilderness wanderings, but by his grace there will be a great deliverance.

V10: The Lord emphasises that even in the days of their wicked rebellion he had adopted various methods of appealing to them by a long line of prophets. Calvin interprets: 'I deposited with them the doctrine which ought to have restored you to the right way . . . I have endeavoured, in every possible way, to restore you to a sound mind.' What aggravated their guilt was that they erred not in ignorance, but in defiance of God and his prophets.

Visions, symbols. The writer to the Hebrews reminds us that in the old days, God had spoken to them at different times, using many different methods of communication (*Heb.* 1:1–3). Though Hosea was one of the earliest of the writing prophets, a long succession of prophets had brought the Lord's message. Since the time of Samuel, there had been Ahijah the Shilonite, Shemaiah, Iddo, Azariah, Hanani, Jehu, Elijah, Elisha, Micaiah, and others not named.

V11: Here is an extended play on words: Gilead, Gilgal, and *gallim* ('piles of stones') all sound very similar. *Aven* may mean iniquity or vanity, and Beth Aven was a common way of referring to Bethel (see 4:15; 5:8; 10:5).

Gilead and Gilgal may represent the two parts of the Northern Kingdom, since Gilead was on the east, and Gilgal on the western side of the Jordan.

The first part of the verse may be read as a question, a dramatic way of emphasising the fact of iniquity in Gilead. Calvin says that the question is ironical. In spite of the abundance of grace and all that God had done to communicate his standards, there was iniquity on every side.

Though they sacrifice bulls. Here, as so often in the prophets, the sacrifices are seen as evidence of empty and sinful worship, outward show devoid of any spiritual content.

Gilgal had been the scene of Israel's rededication when they first crossed the River Jordan, but it had become pre-eminent as a place of idolatry (see 4:15 and 9:15).

Heaps. This may imply that their altars were as common as heaps of stones gathered in the furrows of a field during the ploughing season. Or it may suggest that the altars would be destroyed and become no more than piles of discarded stones.

V12: **Jacob fled to the country of Syria** (NIV: 'Aram'). This proud nation is again reminded of its humble origins. Their ancestor Jacob had been a fugitive, having fled because of his sin. So lowly was his lot that he had to serve for a wife and tend sheep. But God had not abandoned him, and what he became was all by the grace of God. The land in question is probably Aram, the territory between the Tigris and the Euphrates now commonly called Mesopotamia.

V13: **A prophet.** The prophet referred to is Moses (*Deut.* 18:18). It is the prophetic aspect of Moses' ministry that is noted here.

His supreme qualification as the deliverer of God's people was his position as God's spokesman. The instrument God employed was not a king as they desired (*1 Kings* 8:5), but a prophet like many of those messengers whom they had despised and rejected. By a prophet God had made a miserable band of slaves into a nation, bringing it to birth, preserving it, and providing it with an inheritance. The verse also implies a contrast between the hardship of Jacob's lot and the gracious gift of the land they enjoyed.

Preserved, as a flock. Jacob had kept sheep; God had kept Israel. Hosea continually re-emphasises the fact of their dependence on the divine grace.

V14: **Provoked.** Yet in spite of all, Ephraim's rebellion was deep and persistent. They provoked their covenant God, who had revealed himself in such grace, to bitter wrath. Hosea had spoken much about the willingness of God to forgive, but now he declared that God would leave them in their sinful condition because they had so persistently and wilfully rebelled against him.

Therefore his Lord will leave the guilt of his bloodshed upon him. He would have removed the stain of their sin, but they would not turn to him. Their guilt was connected with a whole catalogue of sins, but 'blood guilt' may be applied particularly to murder: those who had died because of oppression, and some who had died as sacrifices to heathen gods (see 13:2).

Return his reproach upon him. The nation would pay for all their sin in the sight of God; the claim of God upon them would never be set aside. As Calvin commented: 'They cannot escape the authority of God, though they have spurned his law' (cf. *Num.* 32:23).

FOR MEDITATION

1. Outline for the chapter: a call to learn spiritual lessons from the past.

  a) The *course that was wrong* (vv1–2). Time and labour were being lavished on vanities.

  b) The *call that was sure* (v6). However mistaken his methods, Jacob valued the inheritance promised to him through Abraham and Isaac. He learned to cling to God and understood at last that the blessing was by favour, not merit.

  c) The *confidence that was false* (vv7–9). Materialism and perverted human cleverness brought arrogance and guilt.

  d) The *challenge that must be faced* (vv10–14). In God's grace, he appealed to them to remember what he had done in giving them the land. He called them to focus on the Word by reminding them of Moses, the prophet. But refusing to listen would bring judgement.

2. Ch 11v12: This may be viewed as drawing a contrast between Israel's apostasy and Judah's relative faithfulness. If the last part of the verse speaks of the uncertainty of Judah's allegiance, we are warned that things may look well on the outside long after corruption has taken hold of the heart. We are reminded that each of us shall be weighed in the balances (*Dan.* 5:25–28). We must examine ourselves (*2 Cor.* 13:5), and pray humbly that the Lord will search our heart to show us what he sees. Shall we be approved or found wanting?

3. Ch 12v1: *Feeding on wind.* Am I trusting in man, material things or false religion, rather than the living God (*Jer.* 17:5–8)? In practical terms, do I keep my word? Can my promises be trusted?

4. Egypt and Assyria were the great powers of the day to which Israel turned for help. But they had no love or concern for

Israel. They cared only about what they could gain for themselves and would not tolerate anyone getting in their way. Such can be the friendship of the world, as the prodigal son in Jesus' parable discovered. Contrast the love of God, who gave the Lord Jesus Christ while we were yet sinners (*Rom.* 5:8); and the Son of God, who gave himself on the cross in our place (*Gal.* 2:20).

At the human level, we are advised to choose our friends with care (*Prov.* 18:24).

5. The earnestness of Jacob should give us an example. For so long he pursued the promises by wrong means, yet he assessed them rightly and desired them earnestly. Jesus commands: 'Seek first the kingdom of God and His righteousness' (*Matt.* 6:33) and directs us that 'where your treasure is, there your heart will be' (*Matt.* 6:21). We may well imitate Jacob's aspirations without employing his methods!

6. Vv3–6: While observing Jacob's enthusiasm for the blessing, we need to bear in mind that he did not earn it by his efforts, which in general hindered more than helped. It was not Jacob who found God, but God who found Jacob. The ladder he saw was let down from heaven (*John* 1:51), not reared up from the earth. The Son of God came down from heaven to lift men up to God: he is the true ladder. Independent human efforts to reach heaven are demonstrated by the Tower of Babel. What trouble that brought! In your heavenward quest, do you have the right ladder?

7. Jacob also gives us a lesson on prevailing prayer. It was the helpless prayer of a crippled man that prevailed at last with God (*James* 5:17). God may have to 'cripple' us with certain disciplines in order to bless us in our intercessions! Are we prepared to wrestle in dependence upon God?

8. V7: Degenerate Israel had become a 'merchant'. They had become like the Canaanites they had been commanded to drive out of the land and destroy. Wealth had become their God, and they had made merchandise of the divine promises. They were behaving more like sons of Esau, who had bargained away the birthright for a bowl of stew, than like sons of Jacob.

What of us? What use are we making of our gospel freedom, our high standard of living in the West, our leisure time, and our knowledge of the gospel? Are we lazy, selfish, materialistically minded Christians?

A challenging illustration is provided by an imaginary conversation in heaven, when the Lord Jesus returned from the earth to his Father. One of the angels asked what he had given to those he had left behind to complete the work. 'I have given them my glory,' said Jesus (*John* 17:22); and the angel asked, 'What have they done with it?' It is but an illustration, but what a telling truth. He has given us his glory. What have we done with it?

9. V10: The variety of methods God uses to reach his people shows both the greatness of his love and the depth of his wisdom and understanding. He persevered in spite of their obtuseness, fitting his words to their state and bearing gently with their stubborn ignorance, yet not denying the requirements of his holiness. He does not change (*Mal.* 3:6), and we should take encouragement from that. We should also be trying to win men and women by every scriptural means, with love, patience, diligence and wisdom.

10. Vv11 and 14: It is often alleged that any religion is better than none, and that it does not really matter what you believe. Clearly God does not agree. Empty religious forms, far from being simply 'not the best', are positively evil. Israel's problem lay squarely in their rejection of the way God himself had

appointed. Have we received God's appointed way? Unless we know redeeming grace through the Lord Jesus Christ, we are left with our blood guilt upon us, and the penalty will one day be required of us. Our prime need is for the One who has been provided by God to meet our need (*Acts* 4:12). Do we regulate our worship by his Word?

12. Vv12 and 13: The *shepherd.*

a) Jacob tended sheep; God tended Jacob. At the end of his long life, Jacob says, 'The God who has fed me all my life long' (*Gen.* 48:15). He too had learned from his personal experience, that God was his shepherd. In pronouncing his final blessing upon his sons, he speaks of a shepherd in a remarkable prophecy, looking forward to the Messiah (*Gen.* 49:24).

b) Moses spent years in the wilderness as a shepherd, and when he led the nation under God, he was very much their shepherd. When he spoke with the Lord about a successor, he expressed his thought in terms of a shepherd (*Num.* 27:17). Jesus echoes Moses' phrase, 'like sheep having no shepherd' (*Matt.* 9:36).

c) David was a shepherd boy when he became the champion of Israel. Later in his reflections he could say, 'The LORD *is* my shepherd' (*Psa.* 23). He who had defended his flock from the lion and the bear was speaking these words from personal experience.

d) Isaiah spoke of the shepherd messianically: 'He will feed His flock like a shepherd' (*Isa.* 40:11). He views God's people as sheep going astray (*Isa.* 53:6).

e) God pronounces that he himself will gather his scattered sheep and bring judgement on those who had failed as shepherds to care for them (*Ezek.* 34).

f) The prophecy of the 'stricken shepherd' (*Zech.* 13:7) was applied by Jesus to himself when he was arrested (*Matt.* 26:31). He gave his life for the sheep (*John* 10:11).

g) In the Psalms, the Lord is the shepherd of his people (*Psa.* 80:1), and the people are 'the people of His pasture, and the sheep of His hand' (*Psa.* 95:7). Wise sheep follow the shepherd.

h) Jesus called himself the shepherd (*John* 10), and later called Peter to tend his sheep (*John* 21:15–17). Peter himself later referred to elders as shepherds (*1 Pet.* 5:2–4).

The metaphor emphasises the vulnerability of men without God. They need a shepherd, and without one they will surely go astray. It emphasises the patient care of God in dealing with the wayward and bringing home the lost. And it points to the Lord Jesus Christ, who saw the crowds as 'sheep having no shepherd' (*Matt.* 9:36) and 'came to seek and to save that which was lost' (*Luke* 19:10).

Finally, the ultimate glory of the 'shepherd' is revealed: 'The Lamb who is in the midst of the throne will shepherd them and lead them' (*Rev.* 7:17). Can one imagine sheep ever complaining that the shepherd does not really understand them, for, after all, he is a man and has never been a sheep? We cannot complain that the One who shepherds us does not understand. We have a shepherd who has been a lamb!

Chapter 13:1–3

The Evil Calf Worship

V1: **When Ephraim spoke, trembling** (NKJ); **When Ephraim spoke, men trembled** (NIV). The first part of the verse offers two possible understandings. The first indicates Ephraim's walk in true fear of God – though it would be difficult to find such a time. The second would indicate the respect in which Ephraim was held. The reign of Jeroboam II would offer such an occasion.

He exalted *himself* in Israel (NKJ); **He was exalted in Israel** (NIV). This second phrase may also be understood in two ways. The tribe of Ephraim, one of the most prominent of the tribes of the Northern Kingdom, was descended from the younger son of Joseph, who was greatly blessed by God. The name means 'doubly fruitful'. It may be noted that Ephraim did show conceits to raise itself among the tribes of Israel in the time of Gideon (*Judg.* 8) and of Jephthah (*Judg.* 12:1). In the rebellion against Rehoboam, son of Solomon, which led to the division of the kingdom, Jeroboam, of the tribe of Ephraim, was the leader of the ten rebellious tribes and became the first king of the separated Northern Kingdom.

When he offended through Baal *worship*. It has been argued that this reference to Baal refers to the apostasy at Baal Peor (*Num.* 25), which exemplified the nation's sin. But it could refer to Jeroboam's institution of the worship of the calves at Bethel and Dan, or to the apostasy in the time of Ahab.

He died. This applies primarily in the spiritual sense. The nation died when it forsook God.

V2: The nation's sin was repeated and aggravated. The silver which had been God's gift to them had been used to make idols, as in a former day, when the trophies taken from Egypt had been willingly given up to make a calf of gold (*Exod.* 32:1–6).

According to their skill. The God-given ingenuity and talent was debased to produce idols. The NIV speaks of 'cleverly fashioned images, all of them the work of craftsmen'. How foolish to worship the work of their own hands, however skilful the work may be!

The AV (and NASB note) 'according to their understanding', stresses the idolatry in the heart of man who has turned to his own way. True religion is by divine revelation, not by human ingenuity (*Prov.* 3:5–6). The Hebrew word usually has a wider meaning than 'skill'. It is the word used of Bezalel and Oholiab, who employed their God-given skill and understanding in the construction of the tabernacles and its furnishings (*Exod.* 36). The Israelites of Hosea's day may be contrasted with them. Rather than building for the glory of God, the Israelites used their skill and understanding to make images for themselves.

The last phrase of the verse also presents difficulty for commentators.

Kiss the calves simply means 'offering them allegiance'. But is there a reference to human sacrifice in the last part of the phrase? The NIV reads 'they offer human sacrifice'; this is included in the margin of some NKJ Bibles. Calvin also took this view. There is no evidence of human sacrifice at either Bethel or Dan, but the argument from silence is dangerous, and the plain sense of the Hebrew is 'they sacrifice men'. The notes of some NASB editions have 'sacrificers of men' or 'sacrificers among men'. Human sacrifice was practised in Judah during the reign of Ahaz in this same period (*2 Chron.* 28:3). Whether they practised human sacrifice or not, their oppression of the poor, stemming from their allegiance to false gods, caused lives to be lost, as is reflected in Amos 4:1 and 5:11–12.

V3: Earlier in the prophecy Hosea had referred to their goodness as a morning cloud and early dew (6:4). Here the phrase expresses the certainty of their being swept away. In four vivid images the prophet shows how quickly they will perish. One is reminded that in the final analysis before God, a nation is no more than its loyalty to God, expressed in its morals. This truth should give the contemporary Western world pause for thought.

FOR MEDITATION

1. 'Before honor *is* humility' (*Prov.* 15:33). When Ephraim had walked with God, he prospered! When we humble ourselves under the mighty hand of God, he will exalt us in due time (*1 Pet.* 5:6). In the words of an old hymn:

> *Fear him, ye saints, and you will then*
> *Have nothing else to fear.*

The trouble began when Ephraim put on pretensions to importance. That is not the way to greatness in the sight of God. We need to pay attention to the teaching and example of the Lord Jesus Christ (*Mark* 10:43–45, *John* 13) and to Paul (*Phil.* 2:3–5).

2. The wages of sin is death. The sinner is already 'dead' (*Eph.* 2:1), although the physical sentence has not yet been exercised. Powerless to help ourselves, we are dependent upon the grace of God in the Lord Jesus Christ. As Charles Wesley put it:

> *'Power into strengthless souls he speaks,*
> *And life into the dead.'*

It is mercy we need, not justice. A story is told of an eminent lady who challenged the artist who had painted her portrait: 'You have not done me justice!' The artist replied, 'Lady, it is mercy you need, not justice.' Whether the story is true, I do not know, but it describes where we all stand in relation to God.

Justice must condemn us; mercy alone can save (*Gal.* 3:10, 13).

[193]

3. V2: *According to their own understanding.* The AV preserves an important truth about the human condition. The faculties given to us by God have been prostituted to the will of self. Our understanding, darkened by sin (*Eph.* 4:18), will inevitably lead us into some form of idolatry (*Rom.* 1:21–23). We need renewal by divine grace before we can begin to think straight (*Eph.* 4:21–24). Without this grace we will use God-given skills to wrong ends. May we learn from Oholiab and Bezalel to use our talents and abilities for his work, to glorify him!

4. The folly of idolatry is brought home to us as we think of giving the kiss of allegiance to man-made calves. Are our idols any more logical? Do I worship the creature and what he makes, rather than the creator? The media idols of the contemporary pop culture, cinema, television or sport and the more sophisticated idols of scientific achievement, politics, philosophy, and even man-centred religion are all doomed to pass away. Only in God may we know eternal life (*Matt.* 6:19–21).

5. The possible reference to human sacrifice challenges us in our own 'enlightened and civilised' society. For the sake of convenience, millions of unborn infants are aborted. In the interests of financial gain, many die from working in foul and polluted conditions or from the effects of sub-standard articles and the products of the tobacco industry. Euthanasia is being considered as a valid way of dealing with 'unwanted lives'. Millions die through wars, purges or oppression. Lives are continually sacrificed in the quest for fulfilment in the drug culture. Even more serious is the spiritual consequence of the philosophy of life that rejects the authority of God and his Word and leads mankind to eternal ruin.

6. Unless my life is centred in the Lord Jesus Christ, I, too, am as a 'morning mist', as chaff or smoke blown in the wind! Our

present earthly life is no more than a vapour that will soon vanish away (*James* 4:14). Apart from God's gift of salvation in the Lord Jesus Christ, the judgement of God will one day carry us away like chaff in the wind (*Matt.* 3:12). Perhaps we need to ask ourselves whether our goodness has that tell-tale quality of vanishing like the morning dew. Am I really a child of grace whose fruit will remain (*John* 15:16)?

7. We need to weigh the truth that 'a nation is no greater than its morals'. What sort of contribution do we make to the nation's morals by our prayers, testimony, example and protest? I am reminded of the sojourn of Lot in Sodom. Truly the Lord declared him 'righteous' (*2 Pet.* 2:7), but his influence and witness counted for little. He had to be constrained by an angel to leave Sodom (*Gen.* 19:18). When he warned his sons-in-law of their danger, they thought that he was joking. His wife was lost and his daughters were tainted. Of what worth was his worldly life? The Apostle Paul speaks of those who are saved, but only as one escaping through the flames (*1 Cor.* 3:15). One can scarcely imagine a believer who would be content with that!

Chapter 13:4–11

The God of Grace Will Act in Wrath

V4: The faithfulness of God is set in contrast to their behaviour. (The verse is reproduced exactly in Isaiah 43:11.) The Jews had known the faithfulness of God continually since the time he had brought them out of Egypt. Experience should have confirmed the conviction that there was no other saviour. In context, the verse may be seen as both a threat and a promise. If they turned away from God there was no other hand to save them. But if they turned again to him, they would discover him to be the same faithful saviour he had always been, however hopeless the situation appeared to be. God is still the only saviour, whatever men may promise or pretend.

V5: **I knew you in the wilderness** (NIV: 'I cared for you in the desert'). 'Cared for' reflects the Septuagint's 'shepherd', expressing choice and care (cf. *Psa.* 144:3). He had brought them through the most arduous wilderness conditions in safety, so that they might understand that they would not have survived but for his grace. In the light of that blessed care, their rebellion is seen as the more sinful. Calvin comments that 'the extreme impiety of the people is here manifestly proved; for having been taught in God's law and been encouraged by so many benefits, they yet went astray after profane superstitions.'

V6: **Filled.** Even in the land of burning heat, they had been brought into rich and fertile pastures where they were amply provided for. Yet in their plenty, they had become proud and self-sufficient and had forgotten God (cf. *Deut.* 8:11–18; 32:15).

V7: Since they had not responded to him with appreciative love, they would meet him in judgement. The lion doubtless suggests the idea of strength and ferocity, and the leopard, swiftness and alertness.

V8: The threefold symbolism vividly depicts the reaction of offended holiness. Some people are offended by such strong language, perhaps because they have little conception of the sinfulness of their sin and the outrage of holy love that is persistently abused and rejected.

V9: Modern translations give different readings for this verse (the NASB offers both alternatives):

   a) **O Israel, you are destroyed, but your help *is* from Me** (NKJ). This translation points them back to him who is their help in their distress.

   b) **I will destroy you, O Israel, because you are against me, against your helper** (NIV). According to this reading, they are reminded that their distress is self-inflicted. They have turned against the Lord, who was their helper.

   Both readings convey vital truth. God did not create mankind, or Israel as a nation, in order to destroy them (*Ezek.* 18:4, 23), and he still calls them to repent (*Ezek.* 18:30–32).

V10: **Where is *any other* [king] that he may save you?** The NIV and NASB follow the Septuagint and the Vulgate. Perhaps this is a reminder of their first rebellious request for a king (*1 Sam.* 8:6). They had made their foolish request; what good had it brought them? This may also be a play on the name of the last king of Israel, Hoshea, meaning 'God is salvation'.

I will be your king (NKJ). It is true that the Lord is ruler over all and particularly king over Israel; his purposes will be accomplished at last. But many Hebrew scholars find this an impossible reading.

V11: Israel had got what they asked for, and they were reaping the consequences of their foolish demands. The idea of continuity is expressed: 'I have been giving you kings.' But ultimately they could not escape God their king, who was able to take away their human kings in his wrath. Men cannot finally escape the judgement of God for their rebellion against him.

FOR MEDITATION

1. V4 suggests three important truths:
   a) The Lord has revealed himself in history, and that as saviour.
   b) He has given his unchanging law: you shall have no other Gods before me.
   c) The Lord is the key to their destiny. He has proved his love for them in redeeming them from Egypt.

God is rich in mercy in the Lord Jesus Christ (*Eph.* 2:4). We are encouraged to seek his mercy (*Isa.* 55:6–7).

2. V6: *Their heart was exalted.* Unfortunately, many believers are like Uzziah (*2 Chron.* 26:15–16). They are greatly helped, but then they become wise in their own conceits, and pride and self-sufficiency set in. We need to bear in mind constantly that we have nothing that we have not received (*1 Cor.* 4:7). Jesus' parable of the rich fool (*Luke* 12) again illustrates the perils and snares of material prosperity.

3. From the time of Moses (*Deut.* 8:11–18) the prophets warned of the dangers of forgetting God. The waywardness of the

human heart (*Jer.* 17:9) must be matched by our watchfulness in employing the means God has given to build up our faith (*Josh.* 1:7–9). Neglect of God's salvation is the initial peril which leads at last to apostasy (*Heb.* 2:1–3).

4. Vv7–8: Lion, leopard, bear, and wild beast all emphasise the strength and the inescapable nature of the divine anger. Yet this is not the caprice of fury and evil temper, but the measured reaction of outraged holiness and despised love. The God who had cared for them in the wilderness as a shepherd, would be to them as the very enemies from whom he had formerly protected them.

When one considers Israel's behaviour and its consequences, one can see why sin and folly are equated in the Scriptures. How foolish to forsake the fountain of living waters, to wear oneself out in pursuit of broken cisterns which cannot hold water (*Jer.* 2:13)! Rejection of God is always self-destructive. He alone can save us from ourselves.

We may at this moment be on such a course – by neglect or laziness, by wilful rejection of God's Word, by casting aside the divine law and refusing to heed the heavenly warnings. Paul could say that he was not disobedient to the heavenly vision (*Acts* 26:19), but we may well ask ourselves whether we have ever seen the vision!

5. Are there other 'kings' in my life from whom I am pursuing satisfaction? Let the glorying of the Christian rest in what he knows of God (*Jer.* 9:23–24, *1 Cor.* 1:31, *2 Cor.* 10:17, *Gal.* 6:14).

6. Israel had first received a king in response to their earnest pleas to Samuel, the man of God, in spite of his warnings about the folly of what they were insisting upon. The step brought them no joy! Matthew Henry comments that 'God often gives us in anger what we sinfully and inordinately desire, gives it

with a curse, and with it, gives us up to our heart's lusts . . .
What we inordinately desire, we are commonly disappointed
in. What he gives us in anger he takes away in wrath; what he
gives us because we did not desire it well, he takes away because
we did not use it well.'

The folly of irresponsible praying is also demonstrated in
Psalm 106:14–15. The phrase 'leanness of soul' (NKJ and
NASB) should prompt us to ask, 'What good is a sleek body if
the soul is lean?'

STUDY TWENTY-THREE

Chapter 13:12–16

Disaster and Deliverance

The passage emphasises the inevitable judgement of Ephraim. But in the middle comes a word of hope so strange to the context that many scholars have attempted to remove it. In truth, though, this is a vital aspect of the divine revelation. The grace of God shines out in an otherwise dark and forbidding sky, offering hope amid the portent of disaster.

V12: **Iniquity** (NIV: 'guilt'). The word seems to apply consistently to the perverseness of sin, rather than to its guilt only (see 4:8; 5:5; 7:1; 8:13; 9:7, 9; 13:12; 14:1–2). Their perverseness was, as it were, stored up in a bag waiting for the day of accounting. The books of God are an infallible and inescapable accuser, a completely just and detailed account of the prosecution's case – a frightening thought when we remember that the prosecutor is one who is of 'purer eyes than to behold evil' (*Hab.* 1:13).

V13: The punishment to come upon Israel is likened to the pains of childbirth. The suggestion of much pain but no birth is found elsewhere (*2 Kings* 19:3, *Isa.* 37:3). Calvin comments: 'They made no effort to obtain the wished-for end to their evils. For when the Lord afflicts us and we bring forth, this bringing forth is our deliverance. Now, how can there be deliverance, except we hate ourselves for our sins, except we raise up our minds to God, and thus open a passage for God's grace?'

This imagery affords some comfort, since childbirth is intended not for destruction but for the propagation of new life. Paul uses this aspect of the analogy (*Gal.* 4:19). The pains are intended to lead to repentance, apart from which there can be no deliverance. At this moment, it seemed to Hosea, there were the pains, but no thought of repentance.

The last part provides a striking similitude of a child lingering at the thought of being born, even though the mother's birth pangs put pressure on the child. In those days a delayed birth was always dangerous.

V14: Modern translations render this in various ways:

The NKJ has four affirmations, concluding with, 'O death, I will be your plagues! O grave, I will be your destruction!' The NIV treats the second part as two questions: 'Where, O death, are your plagues? Where, O grave, is your destruction?' The question form of the last two statements is supported by Paul's quotation (*1 Cor.* 15:54–55), where they are used as an affirmation of victory, not an expression of doubt. The RSV has four questions, but nothing in the Hebrew supports this.

A problem for some commentators is the rapid transition from threat (13:9–13; 15–16) to promise, but this in not unusual in the prophetic writings.

The last phrase has also been variously translated: 'Pity is hidden from My eyes' (NKJ; similar to NASB); 'I will have no compassion' (NIV). The NIV also links this phrase to the threat that follows. This reading makes fair sense, indicating that the immediate judgement will in no way be rescinded. The future of the nation demands a divine miracle, a resurrection from the dead, (cf. *Ezek.* 37). The fulfilment could be in the return from captivity; in the death and resurrection of the Lord Jesus Christ and the birth of the church; or in an eschatological future.

The AV reads: 'Repentance shall be hid from my eyes.' Calvin takes this to mean that the Lord can see no repentance, but

Theodore Laetsch comments that no condition of human repentance is attached to the promise. 'Repentance' may be 'a change of mind', meaning that God will not change his mind about the threat of judgement or the promise. Both will be fulfilled.

God is saying that the judgement must come (1:5–6; 5:7; 13:3), but he will 'raise them from the dead'. The nation will be resurrected.

Ransom and **redeem** imply deliverance on the basis of a price paid, as when a lamb was offered as a substitute (*Exod.* 13:13). The Lord Jesus took up this idea when he spoke of his giving his life a ransom for many (*Mark* 10:45).

This interpretation of the passage emphasises the greatness of the work that God will do. That which is impossible with men will be accomplished by grace. The implication of verse 4 is made explicit here. There is no possibility of any other Saviour.

V15: The subject again is the immediate judgement. At the time of the prophecy the Northern Kingdom appeared to be as a fruitful tree. But the Lord would send a blasting east wind, which would dry up the land. The play on the name Ephraim is repeated, along with a subtle reference to Assyria as the blasting wind from the east.

Some Hebrew scholars have suggested 'among the reeds' for 'among his brethren' (NASB offers both); but the text as found in NKJ and NIV reflects the blessing of Ephraim (*Gen.* 48:19).

The Lord himself was the true spring and fountain of the nation (*Jer.* 2:13). Apart from him the life of the nation would inevitably run dry. It would be devoid of present satisfaction or future hope.

V16: The awful calamity foretold here did take place. Such atrocities were common in ancient days, and the Assyrians had a reputation for brutality even in their own day. King Sargon's palace in Kharsbad has revealed inscriptions reporting that 27,280 Israelites were taken away captive. The prophet emphasises that the disaster is God's judgement, the consequence of the nation's rebellion against him.

FOR MEDITATION

1. Outline for the whole chapter.
   a) The *recognition* of the reason for their distress (vv1–3): their sinful rebellion and idolatry.
   b) The *reason* their redeemer had turned judge (vv4–8): their wilful apostasy.
   c) The *reckoning* from which they cannot escape (vv9–13): their sin is stored for reckoning.
   d) The *renewal* promised by sovereign grace (v14): only God can deliver from death and the grave.
   e) The *re-affirmation* of immediate judgement (vv15–16): the warning to repent.

2. V12: God speaks the most dreadful words about persistence in sin (*Rom.* 2:5, *2 Pet.* 2:9). If we seek to hide in our sin, God will also hide it – for final judgement! Repentance is called for now, for this is the day of salvation (*2 Cor.* 6:2).

3. V13: We must understand the 'pains of travail' in the Christian life. Even God's disciplines are potentially rich with blessing. They are intended to produce 'the peaceable fruit of righteousness' (*Heb.* 12:11). But our unwillingness to accept God's purposes and the demands he makes upon us will prevent our enjoyment of the fullness of new life. Our wilfulness, neglect and disobedience may lead to spiritual 'still birth'.

The metaphor of childbirth is rich with promise. The groaning and travail of this present life need not be in vain

(*Rom.* 8:18–23). We need to recall this during trying times or when we feel ourselves to be under the chastening hand of God.

The foolish human race prefers to rush down the path to death and hell rather than to yield to God and seek his mercy. God threatens destruction, both to subdue the pride of the human heart and to turn us to consider the victory he offers in the death and resurrection of the Lord Jesus Christ.

4. V14: Even if this is read as a question, we are reminded that God alone has power to ransom from death and hell. For the believer there is no 'impossible situation'. God is working out his purposes; and though he acts in judgement, he has promised that not one true grain of his wheat will be lost (*Amos* 9:9).

Treating the verse as a promise, we see a bright ray of hope shining on a very dark situation. Beyond the cross lies the glory of Easter day, and we may rest secure in the promise that those who suffer with Christ will also reign with him (*2 Tim.* 2:12).

5. God does not 'repent'. He may change the mode of his activity, and in Scripture this might be called 'repenting' (*Gen.* 6:6–7, *1 Sam.* 15:11). But he does not change his sovereign purposes (*Num.* 23:19, *1 Sam.* 15:29, *Rom.* 11:29).

6. V14: *Ransom and redemption.*
   Death and the grave are inescapable (*Heb.* 9:27).
   Self-service salvation is impossible (*Psa.* 49:7–8).
   A heavenly promise is indicated (*Psa.* 49:15).
   Divine grace through Jesus Christ is invincible (*Heb.* 7:25, *John* 10:27–29).

7. V15: *The east wind of God's wrath.* The sinner may enjoy prosperity for a time, but like Jonah's gourd, it soon withers (*Psa.* 37, *Psa.* 73). Ask: Am I living in a fool's paradise, or banking in the wrong currency?

8. V16: This is what happens when men are left to themselves. The withdrawal of divine grace is one of the most awful aspects of God's judgement. Israel foolishly refused to heed God's call to repent. Assyria's cruel treatment of Israel shows the unrestrained violence and sinfulness of the human heart. In the light of this example, we should not wonder at the unbelief and appalling violence of contemporary society. Both display the tragedy of turning away from God. The only answer is a revival of true religion (*Psa.* 85:6), because only God can transform the human heart. 'Show us Your mercy, LORD, and grant us Your salvation' (*Psa.* 85:7) should be the heartfelt prayer of every Christian at this time.

Chapter 14:1–9

Israel's Conversion and Renewal

V1: **Return.** The Hebrew verb generally refers not to feelings, but to decisions and to real change in life. It may be argued that this call is effectually directed to the small faithful remnant of the people; even these needed the call to repent. Yet in the broadness of divine mercy, the call was addressed to all, and any who responded in repentance and faith would be received.

You have stumbled. The word conveys the idea of being made feeble, like Samson with his hair shorn. Sin is a stumbling block (*Ezek.* 14:3) which trips us up and makes us weak.

Because of your iniquity. Anyone, to be saved, must accept the divine diagnosis of their trouble and accept the responsibility. The problem is in the heart (*Jer.* 17:9), and only God can cure this perverseness.

V2: **Take words with you.** Hosea calls for confession of sin, in contrast to the meaningless rituals which were masquerading as religion. Turning to God is a conscious and thoughtfully considered matter, not a jumble of emotions.

Notice that it is as though the Lord were putting the words into their mouths. The mystery of the tension between the divine sovereignty and human responsibility is displayed. We are responsible beings, yet the Lord in grace gives all the help we can ever need to appropriate and work out our salvation.

The prophet then specifies the nature of the words required.

Take away all iniquity. The Hebrew word translated 'iniquity' is frequently found in Hosea. In Scripture it generally refers to perverseness, but it can also denote guilt. This acknowledges that God alone can deal with both aspects of the problem. As Toplady states it in the hymn 'Rock of Ages':

Be of sin the double cure,
Cleanse me from its guilt and power.

Every known sin should be confessed without compromise and the divine remedy applied (*1 John* 1:9).

Receive *us* graciously. The Jewish Publications Society reads this as 'accept that which is good' (also offered by the NASB note), which is understood in the light of Isaiah 1:16–19 and Micah 6:8. When the Spirit of God works in a man's heart and he whole-heartedly turns to God, there will be evidence (*Luke* 3:8). Paul teaches that repentance is God's gift (*2 Tim.* 2:25). Calvin reads the phrase as 'bring good', which he regards as a prayer for blessing: 'First receive us into favour and then prove in reality that thou art propitious to us, even by outward benefits.'

For we will offer the sacrifices of our lips (NIV, NASB: 'fruit'). The word translated 'sacrifices' or 'fruit' literally means 'bull calves' (hence AV: 'the calves of our lips'), indicating a costly offering. In this context it means 'words of worship acceptable to God' (cf. *Psa.* 69:30–31, *Heb.* 13:15). Calvin brings out the sense of wonder that we can do nothing to return to God except to celebrate his goodness.

V3: **Assyria shall not save us.** Assyria was the power to which Hoshea and his party had been looking for aid. Some understand the phrase as the prophet's warning and pleading with the nation. Others see it as part of Israel's acceptable confession that they would no longer trust in the help of foreign powers.

We will not ride on horses. Egypt was a great source of the most highly bred horses (*1 Kings* 10:28). This may represent the repentance of those who looked to Egypt rather than to Assyria for help. Or it may be a pledge that warlike power, symbolised by horses, would no longer be trusted.

Nor will we say anymore to the work of our hands. Israel completely renounces idolatry, throughly recognising that salvation would be solely the work of God, and not due either to Assyrian or Egyptian help, or to Israel's own efforts and idolatrous paraphernalia. After the return of Judah from captivity in Babylon, the Jews completely renounced idolatry.

For in You the fatherless finds mercy (cf. *Psa.* 10:14). When they turn to God, those who have been forsaken by every other helper find the steadfast love of a caring father, as did the prodigal son. Hosea had already described this overflowing mercy of God (2:23).

V4: **I will heal their backsliding** (NIV: 'waywardness'). God alone can deal with the faithlessness of the human heart. Here is the substance of the new covenant later expounded by Jeremiah (31:33–34) and Ezekiel (36:26). The stony heart is taken away and a tender responsive heart given.

I will love them freely. God's love is directed by his grace alone and does not rest on any merit in the recipient. As Charles Wesley put it in one of his hymns: 'He has loved, he has loved us, because he would love.' That free love causes his anger to be turned away by his provision of the all-sufficient ransom of Christ, the one who had no sin made sin for us (*2 Cor.* 5:21)

My anger has turned away (cf. *Mic.* 7:17–18, *1 Pet.* 2:24). The awesome nature of the divine wrath has been made very clear in 13:1–11, and the necessity of redemption and ransom is expressed in 13:14.

God, through the sacrifice of his beloved Son, has accomplished that which was impossible with man. Anger has been turned away because God has provided a ransom in giving his Son to be the Redeemer. This short phrase exalts the grace and righteousness of God in the redemption of sinners (*Isa.* 53:6).

In subscribing to that mighty truth, we must not think of the Lord Jesus as an unwilling victim. The writer to the Hebrews speaks of the 'blood of the eternal covenant', reminding us that the Father and the Son entered in eternity into this covenant, whereby the Son willingly became the redeemer of the church.

V5: This outpouring of the Lord's love will bring great blessing to Israel (cf. *Jer.* 17:5–8). A contrast to 13:15 may be intended. One who turns away from God is going out into the wilderness, but one who turns to God becomes like a tree planted by streams of water (cf. *Psa.* 1:3, *Isa.* 48:17–18; 58:11).

I will be like the dew. This symbolises gentle, refreshing, life-giving grace.

He shall grow like the lily. The lily is a symbol of fruitfulness (*Isa.*27:6). Pliny spoke of the lily of Palestine as unsurpassed in its fecundity, often producing fifty bulbs from a single root. Calvin wrote that the lily grew swiftly, 'rising in one night'. He also notes that the imagery of the lily and of Lebanon speaks of the suddenness and enduring nature of the divine blessing.

Roots like Lebanon symbolises strength and stability. The Lord himself, the everlasting Rock, is the believer's stability (*Isa.* 26:4).

V6: **His branches shall spread** (NIV, NASB: 'shoots'). This may express the idea of a multitude of new shoots from the root (cf. *Isa.* 11:1; 53:2), or tall leafy cedars of Lebanon providing shade from the heat.

His beauty shall be like an olive tree. This depicts fruitfulness. The olive yards were an essential part of Israel's economy.

His fragrance like Lebanon. The clear mountain air carries the scent of the pine forests, and the lower slopes are clothed with aromatic shrubs: lavenders, myrtle, and fragrant reeds. This may reflect 'a sweet-smelling aroma, an acceptable sacrifice, well pleasing to God' (*Phil.* 4:18; cf. *2 Cor.* 2:14).

V7: **Those who dwell under his shadow shall return** (NKJ); 'Men will again dwell in his shade' (NIV). Some see a reference to the blessedness of those who turn to God. Others see a promise that restored Israel will enjoy such blessing that other nations will be blessed through association with them. The last part of the verse speaks of restored fruitfulness. The return to the imagery of the vine sets up a contrast with 10:1.

V8: While the overall sense is clear, the detailed meaning has been approached several ways:

a) This is a dialogue between God and Israel.
Ephraim shall say, What have I to do anymore with idols?
Jehovah: 'I have heard him and observed him.'
Israel: 'I am like a green cypress tree.'
Jehovah: 'Your fruit is found in me.'
According to this interpretation, Ephraim renounces idols. The Lord speaks approvingly of him. Ephraim then speaks of the richness of the new experience, and the Lord reminds him that he is the source of his fruitfulness, to guard his humility.

b) These are all the words of Jehovah: I no longer have to plead with Ephraim about idolatry, and I will concern myself with his destiny. He compares himself with a green cypress tree, and in me he will find his fruitfulness.

c) These are the words of Ephraim. First idols are renounced; then Ephraim professes what he has learned of God in mercy, grace and pardon. The nation is now like a green cypress tree, living under the fruitful riches of the divine blessing, confessing that all the fruit is by the divine grace.

d) Calvin divides the verse into two parts. The first is Israel's renunciation of idols, and the rest is the Lord's promise of blessing to Israel.

However the details of the exposition are handled, the important truths are clear: Israel's renunciation of idols; Jehovah's watchful care and grace upon his people Israel; and the new life that grace has brought to Israel.

V9: The final verse is generally regarded as an epilogue to the whole book.

Who *is* wise? The wise and prudent are expected to understand and heed the message of the prophet.

The ways of the LORD *are* right (cf. *Deut.* 32:4). Some suggest that 'right' here means 'direct', leading straight to the objective, giving peace and satisfaction and leading into fellowship with God. His ways are to be followed with unswerving zeal.

Poole comments: 'The ways which he would have us walk in towards him . . . are all righteous and equal. And the ways wherein God walketh toward us, in correction for sins committed, in suspending his promises of grace, on conditions of duty, in afflicting or comforting, are all righteous and very equal.'

The righteous walk in them. They consent to the justice of God's ways and walk without fear. The righteous are obedient. Love for God means obeying his commands, and his commands are not burdensome (*1 John* 5:3).

But transgressors stumble in them. The sinner continually deviates from the divine standards. He is offended by them and revolts against them.

Christ is to some the Rock on which they depend and are safe (*Isa.* 28:16), while to others he is 'a stone of stumbling and a rock of offence' (*Isa.* 8:14, *1 Pet.* 2:8).

FOR MEDITATION

1. Outline for the chapter:
   a) The *call* to return to God (vv1–3).
   b) The *comfort* of divine grace (vv4–8).
   c) The *challenge* of true wisdom (v9).

2. The devastating threats of the awfulness of divine judgement are followed by a gracious call to repent, reminding us yet again that God does not delight in the death of sinners but is pleased when they turn from their sins and live (*Ezek.* 18:23, 32).

God's call is to a wayward people, and we should note the following aspects of it:

a) God still concerns himself with people who have been so stubborn in their rejection of divine forgiveness. It is pure mercy that God calls anyone to himself. '*Through* the LORD's mercies we are not consumed' (*Lam.* 3:22–24). That should constrain us, when we have fallen, to turn back to him. It also exemplifies the patient compassion we should show to those who seem to be difficult and hopeless cases.

b) He is pleased to address the Israelites as 'their God'. He would identify himself with them even in their sin. The Lord Jesus symbolised the identification with fallen humans in his baptism. Eventually at the cross he fulfilled what his baptism had symbolised and was actually made to be sin for us (*2 Cor.* 5:21). In Hosea, as in the New Testament, the true Israel of God would in their repentance discover that they had really been his all along. It was grace that had brought them home (*Rom.* 8:29).

c) The call to repentance is not merely a call to standards for life, but to a Person. The invitation indicates his willingness to have us, but we must have him as our God and king, loving him with heart and soul and strength (*Deut.* 6:4). Where but in his grace shall we find the resources to aspire to such demands?

> *Thou art the life, to thee alone*
> *From sin and death we flee:*
> *And he who would the Father seek,*
> *Must seek him, Lord, by thee.*
>
> – George Washington Doane

d) We must accept the fact that the cause of our trouble is our sin. We cannot lay the blame on our circumstances, on our environment, or on other people. As Shakespeare put it in *Julius Caesar*: 'The fault, dear Brutus, is not in our stars, but in ourselves that we are underlings.'

3. Vv2–3: Confession (cf. *1 John* 1:9).

a) Petitioning words: we request to be acquitted from guilt, to be accepted as righteous.

b) Promissory words: we give thanks and amend our lives. In our confession of sin, we must be particular. In returning to God and in our renunciation of sin we must covenant particularly against those sins to which we have been most in bondage. When people know themselves to have been forgiven, grace will dispose them to forgive others (*Matt.* 6:2, *Eph.* 4:32).

c) Pleading words: we face up to our natural state as 'orphans'. The request is addressed to the love and pity of God.

'We cannot expect that God will take away sin by forgiving it, unless we put it away by forsaking it' (Matthew Henry).

The Lord Jesus Christ, our Great High Priest, is the one to whom we must turn. His reconciling work on the cross is the full and complete payment for the judgement due to our sins. The resources of his Spirit are sufficient to enable us in the battle against sin. His perfect righteousness is counted to us, so that we may stand spotless before God. Faith is the key to this door of hope.

4. V2: A comment from Richard Sibbes:

> This is for reproof to those who, in their distresses, set their wit, wealth, friends and all a-work, but never set God a-work, as Hezekiah did in Sennacherib's case. The first time he turned him off to his cost, with enduring a heavy taxation, and yet was never a whit better for it (*2 Kings* 18:15), for Sennacherib came shortly after and besieged Jerusalem, until Hezekiah had humbled himself and prayed; and then God chased all away and destroyed them. He had better have done so at first, and so saved his money and pains, too. The like weakness we have a proof of in Asa, who, when a greater army came against him . . . prayed and trusted in God, and so was delivered, with the destruction of his enemies (*2 Chron.* 14:11), yet in lesser danger

against Baasha, king of Israel, distrusted God, and sent out the treasures of the house of God and of his own house, to Ben-hadad, king of Syria, to have help of him by a diverting war against Baasha, which his plot, though it prospered, yet was he reproved by the prophet Hanani, and wars thenceforth denounced him (*2 Chron.* 16). This Asa, notwithstanding this experiment, afterwards sought unto the physician, before he sought unto God (*2 Chron.* 16:12).[1]

We are prone to trust in the arm of flesh, and even those who have learned true faith in God are not above lapsing again into their former folly.

5. V3: The horse was the ultimate deterrent of that time (see *Psa.* 24:7; 33:17, *Prov.* 21:31). The Christian should not put their trust in human devices – 'carnal confidences', the Puritans called them. God alone should be our refuge and strength (*Psa.* 46:1), and our trust should be in the weapons that he provides (*2 Cor.* 10:3–5, *Eph.* 6:10–18).

6. V4: God comes to us with a wondrous offer of redeeming grace. The initiative is his; we can only respond to his goodness.
His promise gives hope: 'I will love them freely.'
His attitude is gracious: 'My anger is turned away.'
His grace is expressed: 'I will heal his waywardness.'

7. Some thoughts from Alexander Maclaren in 'The Dew and the Plants':
'For all life and growth of the spirit, there must be a bedewing from God.' The heavy night clouds bring a heavy and refreshing mist, in contrast to the burning east wind of the previous chapter.

[1] From 'The Returning Backslider', in *Works of Richard Sibbes, Vol.2* (Edinburgh: Banner of Truth, 1983), p.259.

'Be you Israel [wrestling all night in prayer], and God will surely be your dew and life: growth will be possible.'

'A soul thus bedewed by God will spring into purity and beauty . . . Ugly Christianity is not Christ's Christianity: it used to be a favourite saying that unattractive saints had "grace grafted on a crab stick". Paul said "adorn the teaching".'

'The soul that has been made fair and pure by communion with God ought also to be strong.' The firm roots of the cedar are an emblem of stability and vigour. Scripture calls us to be strong in the Lord and in the power of his might.

'The God-bedewed soul, beautiful, pure and strong, will bear fruit.' The beauty is not such as strikes the eye, for the olive tree has a gnarled look, and the fruit is crushed to produce oil.

'Christian people have received all our dew and all our beauty and all our strength that we may give other people light, that we may be the means of conveying to other people nourishment, that we may move gently in the world as lubricating, sweetening, soothing influences. The question is, does anyone gather fruit from us, and would anybody call us trees of righteousness, the planting of the Lord, that he may be glorified?'[2]

8. Vv5–7: The benefits God bestows to and through his church:

The dew speaks of gentle and continuous refreshing. The promise of Jacob (*Gen.* 27:28) is supremely fulfilled in God's giving of himself. It is not just that he gives the dew; he is the dew. With this we may compare the statement of the Lord Jesus (*John* 6:32–40) that he is the bread of life, drawing a distinction between Moses, who was God's agent in providing the manna, and himself, who is the bread.

The consequence is growth in beauty, stability, and fruit-fulness. The church thus blessed becomes a place of shade in

---

[2] From *The Books of Ezekiel, Daniel and the Minor Prophets* (London: Hodder and Stoughton, 1908), pp.134–142.

whose protection its members will thrive as individuals. Isaiah 32:2 will be true of the Lord and his people.

Ask: Am I enjoying the divine sufficiency and producing the expected fruit? Is the church of which I am part a place of shade for Christians and other needy souls, where they find the peace of God to face the storms of life? Are the compassion and strength of Christ found within its fellowship?

9. V7: *The scent of the wine of Lebanon.* As the Lord Jesus turned water into wine, so the dull waters of mere religion become, through grace, rich and sweet like wine. The sullied waters of our old life outside of Christ are transformed to reflect his beauty and grace (*John 2*).

10. Vv4–7: 'We have the answer of peace to the prayers of returning Israel' (Matthew Henry).

Do they dread God's displeasure? He assures them that his anger is turned away from them.

Do they pray for the taking away of all iniquity? He assures them that he will take away all faithlessness, the source of their failure.

Do they pray that God will receive them graciously? He promises to love them freely.

Do they pray that God will do them good? He promises that he will be as the dew to them.

11. *He casts forth his roots as Lebanon.* From a sermon by C.H. Spurgeon:

And let me remind you, my dear friends, that growing downward is a very excellent thing to promote stability. Perhaps that is the exact meaning of the passage. When we are first brought to God, we are like the lily, wafted by the wind; afterwards we grow downwards, and become firm. I am fully convinced that the prevailing lack of this age is not so much in respect to growing upwards as growing downwards . . . The fact is, some of you have no idea of what fundamental truth in theology is. The popular cry is for liberality of sentiment, and if a man happens to say a hard word against anything he thinks essentially wrong, he is accounted a bigot directly. Many of you shrink from the imputation of bigotry, as if it were more awful than heresy in regard to the faith. You would as soon be called a common informer as be called a bigot. I beseech you, do not be appalled at a taunt. Do not be a bigot, but do not be ashamed of being called one. A man ought to have stable principles, and not be ever shifting about from one set of opinions to another. He ought not to be hearing a Calvinistic minister in the morning, and saying that is good, and then going in the evening to hear an Arminian minister, and saying that is good. We are often told by some ministers in their drawing rooms that God will not ask in the day of judgement what a man believed, for if his life has been correct, it will not much matter what doctrines he held. I am at a loss for the authority on which they base such laxness. I wonder who told them that was the truth. I have read my Bible through, and I have never found a text that could absolve my judgment from its allegiance to my Maker. I hold, that to believe wrongly is equally as great a sin in the sight of heaven as to act wrongly. Error is a crime before God, and though there is liberty of conscience, so far as man and man are concerned, there is no liberty of conscience with God. You are not free to believe truth or to believe error just as you like. You are bound to believe what God says is truth, and on your soul's peril be it, that you believe two things that are contrary, or confound the positive and the negative, where faith is the evidence of justification, and unbelief the seal of a sinner's doom. Methinks God will say to you at last, 'Man, I gave thee brains: I endowed thee with reason; how couldst thou suppose thyself less responsible for the use of thy brains than for the use of thy tongue?' One man says 'yes', and another 'no'; and because it is the fashion to call out 'Liberality, liberality, liberality', thou dost assent to both; and joining the crowd, thou art sincere in neither. Thou oughtest rather to say, 'I believe that what I hold is true, and if I did not I should not avow it; and believing it to be true, I cannot hold that the opposite is true, nor can I be continually going to hear one doctrine at one time and another at another. My conscience demands that I distinguish between things that differ.'[3]

12. Vv 5–7: In the same sermon, Spurgeon continues to speak on the various effects of grace in the human heart.

Well, what next? After the Christian has become confirmed in his doctrine, and has received the truth in the love of it, what next? Why, the next thing is he makes a profession! 'His branches shall spread'. . . He says, 'I am a Christian, I cannot keep it a secret'. . .

Having joined a church and made a profession, what is the next effect of grace for the believer then? Why it is to make him beautiful as 'the olive tree'. . . Again, 'his smell shall be as Lebanon'. Now, I take it 'the smell' means the report which will go out concerning a man . . . Without seeking for it, he will obtain a blessed name among his brethren, and some name also amongst the world . . .

In one of Whitefield's sermons he speaks of some young man who said, 'I will not live in my old father's house, for there is no chair or table there but smells of his piety.' That is what you should endeavour to do, to make your house so smell of piety that the wicked man cannot stop in . . . and it may be said of you, 'Ah! he was one who reflected his Master's image, and who sought to adorn the doctrine of God his Saviour in all things.'[4]

[3] From 'Grace Reviving Israel', No 342, in *The New Park Street Pulpit, Containing Sermons of the Rev C H Spurgeon, Vol. VI* (London: Passmore & Alabaster, 1860), p.448.
[4] pp.449–50, 452.

Ask: Am I committed to God to make me such a person, ready to prove the good and acceptable and perfect will of God (*Rom.* 12:2)?

13. To stir our poor divided hearts to such a commitment, let us consider a passage from Richard Sibbes, commenting on Hosea 14:

> Mercy is God's sweetest attribute, which sweeteneth all his other attributes; for, but for mercy, whatsoever else is in God were matter of terror to us. His justice would affright us. His holiness likewise (considering our impurity) would drive us from him. 'Depart from me', saith Peter to our Saviour, 'for I am a sinful man' (*Luke* 5:8). And when the prophet Isaiah saw God in his excellency a little, then he said, 'Woe is me, for I am undone, because I am a man of unclean lips' (*Isa.* 6:5). His power is terrible; it would confound us; his majesty astonish us. Oh! but mercy mitigates all. He that is great in majesty, is abounding in mercy; he that hath beams of majesty hath bowels of mercy. Oh! this draweth especially miserable persons.[5]

---

[5] From 'The Returning Backslider', in *Works of Richard Sibbes, Vol. 2*, pp.292–293.

Notes on Authors Cited

Thomas Brooks (1608–80), a Puritan, entered Emmanuel College, Cambridge in 1625 and was ordained to the ministry before 1640. He ministered in London. After being ejected in 1662 he continued to preach there as a non-conformist, and ministered there during the plague when many of the official clergy fled.

John Calvin (1509–64) was a Frenchman whose name is associated with the Reformation in Geneva. Having experienced in about 1533 what he described as a 'sudden conversion', he broke with the Roman Catholic Church and in 1536 published the first edition of *The Institutes of the Christian Religion,* which was a clear defence of Reformation beliefs. In 1537 he was invited to Geneva. Because of bitter opposition there, however, he moved to Strasbourg, but returned to Geneva in 1541 at the insistence of the Council of Citizens. He remained there for the rest of his life, making a deep impact on the life of the city as well as upon individuals. He preached systematically through most of the books of the Bible, and his commentaries are still of great value and relevance today.

John Flavel (1627–91) went to University College, Oxford and into the Church of England ministry in Dartmouth. He was removed in 1662, after Charles II came to the throne, but he continued to preach in his own house and in nearby villages until an Act of Indulgence by James II in 1687 enabled him to return officially to his parish.

Thomas Goodwin (1600–79) was born near Yarmouth and in his teens went to Christ's College, Cambridge. In 1620 he was elected Fellow of St Catherine's Hall. Sometime in this period he experienced deep conviction of sin and was converted. In 1625 he became Preacher to the University and earned a great reputation for his scholarship and eloquence. But his discontent with the Church of England caused him to resign office in 1634 and become an Independent. After spending time in Holland, he returned to London as an Independent pastor. He rose to prominence during the Commonwealth, was appointed to the Westminster Assembly in 1643 and preached often before Cromwell and the Parliament. In 1649 he was made President of Magdalen College, Oxford. At the Restoration in 1660, he returned to London and, despite government restrictions, persevered quietly there as an Independent pastor until his death. He was one of the most influential of the Puritans but remained a humble and caring man in the service of God's people.

Hugh Latimer (c1485–1555) was born near Lutterworth, in Leicestershire. He graduated from Cambridge and was prominent as an orthodox Catholic preacher until his conversion, when he became a fearless Protestant preacher. A man of great ability and sincerity, he attracted the attention of Henry VIII, who made him Bishop of Worcester. When Latimer could not accept the 'Six Articles', which reaffirmed Roman Catholic doctrines, he resigned his bishopric, much to the annoyance of the king. Under Edward VI he exercised much influence, but when Edward died he became a target of Queen Mary's persecuting zeal. In 1555, along with Nicholas Ridley, he was burned at the stake. He is remembered for his famous dying encouragement to Ridley: 'Be of good comfort Master Ridley, and play the man. We shall this day light such a candle, by God's grace, in England, as I trust shall never be put out.'

Alexander Maclaren (1826–1910), was a Scottish Baptist whose ministry began in 1845 in a small church in Portland, in Southampton. In 1858 he was called to the Union Chapel in Manchester, where his preaching ministry became famous and lasted for forty-five years. Though hailed as 'a prince of preachers', he was a self-effacing man who often suffered from 'stage fright'. His *Expositions* were a famous preaching resource in the early part of the twentieth century.

Henry Scougal (1650–78), the son of a bishop of Aberdeen, was distinguished in his own day for his godliness and scholarship. He became professor of philosophy at King's College Aberdeen in his nineteenth year. His little book *The Life of God in the Soul of Man* was first published in 1677 in London and by 1733 had gone through six impressions. It had a profound spiritual impact on both Charles Wesley and George Whitefield and continues to be a challenge today.

Richard Sibbes (1577–1635) was born in Tostock, Suffolk. He entered St John's College, Cambridge, in 1595 and was converted under the preaching of Paul Bayne, the successor of William Perkins, at Great St Andrew's Church. He became Lecturer at Holy Trinity Church, Cambridge. From 1617 to 1626 he preached at Gray's Inn, London, returning to Cambridge when he became Master of Catherine Hall. He also returned to Holy Trinity as its vicar. No compromiser of truth, he was reprimanded for his boldness in 1627. Five years later he and eleven other Puritan ministers were sentenced to banishment, but the sentence was never carried out. He did, however, see many of his good friends, including Thomas Goodwin, imprisoned or forced to emigrate. Sibbes is among the most significant of the Puritan preachers, his sermons and other works combining strength, simplicity and depth. He was known to his contemporaries as 'the sweet dropper' and 'the heavenly Dr Sibbes'.

C.H. Spurgeon (1834–92) became the minister of New Park Street in London, a famous old Baptist Church, at the age of nineteen. The church, with its seating capacity of some 4000, soon overflowed. A new church, the Metropolitan Tabernacle, opened in 1861 with a seating capacity of 6000. Almshouses, an orphanage and a 'preachers' college' demonstrate the diversity of Spurgeon's gospel work. A prominent means of outreach was the publishing of weekly sermons, known as 'The New Park Street Pulpit' (1855–1860) and 'The Metropolitan Tabernacle Pulpit' (1861–1917), the sermons continuing to be published long after his death. He was also the author of many important books and pamphlets. In 1887 he withdrew from the Baptist Union during a long and bitter battle known as 'The Downgrade Controversy'. Spurgeon was concerned that the Union was departing from commitment to the authority of the Scriptures.

James Hudson Taylor (1832–1905) was a Yorkshire man who became an outstanding missionary pioneer and statesman. In 1865 he founded the China Inland Mission, now known as the Overseas Missionary Fellowship, which works throughout southeast Asia. His devotion and self-sacrifice are exemplary, especially to the young, for he began to prepare himself for what he believed to be the call of God whilst he was still in his teens, beginning a lifelong commitment in which he unremittingly persevered.

All these men were bold defenders of the faith, whose works are worthy of our reading and whose examples should inspire and encourage us.

SOME OTHER
BANNER OF TRUTH
TITLES

THE ROARING OF THE LION
A Commentary on Amos

Ray Beeley

The prophecy of Amos begins 'two years before the earthquake'. Everyone in the prophet's time remembered the earthquake. It must have come unexpectedly and shaken the earth, destroying buildings with irresistible force. In a few never-to-be-forgotten moments, ancient grandeur became rubble, leaving even the people of God stunned.

But the earthquake was only physical. Two years before a warning of a deeper shaking of the foundations had been given by an obscure farmer from the highlands of Tekoa. Amos appeared to announce a more threatening sound – the voice of God. The roar of the Divine Lion sounded. Amos heard it and was compelled to prophesy. His words of judgment on the nations and on the professing church echo through the centuries with permanent relevance. Will what has been built in the churches stand the test?

Ray Beeley's guide to Amos reflects both his own love of Scripture and the gifts he exercised prior to his retirement as a Head Teacher of Religious Knowledge and minister of Richmond Wesleyan Reform Church, Yorkshire.

ISBN: 0 85151 715 3
128 pp. Paperback
£3.95/$7.99

HOSEA
Commentary on the
Minor Prophets, Vol. 1

John Calvin

The first of the five volumes of Calvin's *Commentary on the Minor Prophets,* and still acknowledged to be of great value, even in a day when commentaries on Scripture abound. All of Calvin's commentaries stand out as models of honesty, good sense and evangelical warmth.

His great gifts as an interpreter of Scripture are clearly evident in his treatment of the often-neglected Minor Prophets. He opens up the rich contents of these books to our hearts and minds, clearly explaining their teaching concerning false religion, spiritual adultery, injustice, judgement, the remnant, the promise of restoration, and the outworkings of sovereign grace and love.

ISBN: 0 85151 473 1
544 pp. Clothbound
£10.95/$22.99

PRECIOUS REMEDIES AGAINST SATAN'S DEVICES

Thomas Brooks

Thomas Brooks (1608–80) was educated, like many of his Puritan contemporaries, at Emmanuel College, Cambridge. Much of his subsequent ministry was exercised in various London parishes. The first fruit of his preaching and writing to be published was *Precious Remedies Against Satan's Devices* in 1652. Here he deals very thoroughfully and helpfully with the opposition the people of God meet with from the devil and explains the remedies which Scripture provides to meet these assaults.

The Trust also publishes his famous work on assurance, *Heaven on Earth* (ISBN 0 85151 356 5, 320 pp. paperback, £4.50/$8.99) and his *Works* in six volumes.

ISBN 0 85151 002 7
256 pp. Paperback
£3.50/$7.50

THE BRUISED REED

Richard Sibbes

In his famous exposition of Isaiah 42:3 and Matthew 12:20, *The Bruised Reed and the Smoking Flax,* Richard Sibbes unfolds the tender ministry of Jesus Christ, who is 'a physician good at all diseases, especially at the binding up of the broken heart'. The republication of this masterpiece of experimental godliness has been widely welcomed. A reviewer has said that Sibbes 'shows a deep and sensitive understanding of the many doubts, fears, failures and struggles which so often trouble Christians The book is full of godly realism . . . Sibbes shows us a gentle, compassionate Christ, who loves and protects his people.'

The Trust also publishes *Glorious Freedom* (ISBN 0 85151 791 9, 196 pp. paperback, £2.95/$5.99), a very helpful work on the believer's liberty in Christ, based on 2 Corinthians 3:17–18), and Sibbes' *Works* in seven volumes.

ISBN 0 85151 740 4
138 pp. Paperback
£2.50/$4.99

THE WORKS OF JOHN FLAVEL
(Six-Volume Set)

John Flavel (1628–91), the son of a Puritan minister who died in prison for his non-conformity, was educated at University College, Oxford, and laboured for almost the whole of his ministry at Dartmouth in Devon. Much of his preaching was to seafarers, and this is reflected in such sermons as *Navigation Spiritualized* and *The Seaman's Companion* in Volume 5 of this set. In addition to numerous sermons, the set also contains such notable works as *The Fountain of Life: A Display of Christ in His Essential and Mediatorial Glory, Pneumatologia: A Treatise of the the Soul of Man, Divine Conduct, or the Mystery of Providence,* and *Twelve Sacramental Meditations.* The Trust also publishes his *Divine Conduct* separately in the Puritan Paperbacks series as *The Mystery of Providence* (ISBN: 0 85151 104 X, 224 pp., £3.25/ $6.99)

ISBN: 0 85151 060 4
6 Volumes,
clothbound
£84.95/$174.99

For free illustrated catalogue please write to
THE BANNER OF TRUTH TRUST
3 Murrayfield Road, Edinburgh EH12 6EL, UK
P O Box 621, Carlisle, Pennsylvania 17013, USA